NO LONGER PROPERTY OF
ANYTHINK LIBRARIES
DISTRICT

D0118981

THE one-pot gourmet gardener

Delicious container recipes to
grow together and cook together

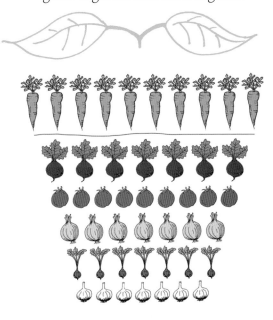

THE one-pot gourmet gardener

Delicious container recipes to
grow together and cook together

CINEAD McTERNAN

PHOTOGRAPHY BY JASON INGRAM

F

FRANCES LINCOLN LIMITED
PUBLISHERS

Frances Lincoln Limited
74–77 White Lion Street
London N1 9PF
www.franceslincoln.com

The One-pot Gourmet Gardener
Copyright © Frances Lincoln
    Limited 2015
Text copyright © Cinead
    McTernan 2015
Photographs copyright
    © Jason Ingram 2015
Illustrations copyright
    © Becky Clarke

First Frances Lincoln edition
2015

All rights reserved.
No part of this publication
may be reproduced, stored in a
retrieval system, or transmitted,
in any form, or by any means,
electronic, mechanical,
photocopying, recording or
otherwise without the prior
written permission of the
publisher or a licence permitting
restricted copying. In the
United Kingdom such licences
are issued by the Copyright
Licensing Agency, Saffron
House, 6–10 Kirby Street,
London EC1N 8TS.

A catalogue record for this book
is available from the British
Library.

ISBN 978-0-7112-3590-8

Printed and bound in China

1 2 3 4 5 6 7 8 9

CONTENTS

INTRODUCTION

YOU DO NOT NEED TO OWN a wicker basket or rent an allotment plot to grow your own fruit, vegetables and herbs. Picking a home-grown tomato straight off the vine or unearthing a carrot is not just for those who have hectares of space and very green fingers. If you have only a small patio, balcony or roof garden, you can have plenty of success with container-grown crops. Fruit, vegetables and herbs will thrive in pots if given the right position and a bit of care and attention, especially when watering and feeding. These days there are even cultivars of fruit and vegetables that have been bred particularly to cope in pots and still provide bumper crops.

Even if you have room for only one pot, you can still enjoy the experience of growing a crop, caring for it and then harvesting it. And then of course you get to eat it, freshly picked and in season – just as Mother Nature intended. Going out to check what crop is ready to pick is always a thrill and eating it the same day is like having the cherry on the cake.

The unbeatable taste of freshly picked, home-grown produce is a good

reason why growing your own is such a popular pastime, but there are other considerations and benefits too. Home-growing may also be a reaction to the number of air miles involved in stocking our supermarket shelves; in defiance of supermarket buyers who assume we want to buy strawberries out of season; or because tasteless, characterless apples are all that are on offer in late summer and autumn, rather than one of our delicious heritage varieties.

Growing at home also means you know exactly what – or, more to the point, what has not – been sprayed on the produce you are feeding your family. Of course, it is also a huge amount of fun and the ever-growing allotment waiting lists are testament to this general enthusiasm for getting dirt under our fingernails.

Home-grown produce may look a bit more knobbly than their supermarket counterparts, but the taste is far superior. With all the promise of delicious crops on your doorstep, deciding what exactly to grow can pose a dilemma. Some growers suggest sticking to favourite varieties; others recommend growing produce that is expensive to buy; while experienced growers champion the idea of experimenting with unusual crops. All great advice, but it still can be

---

LEFT Fresh and in season! Chard is a late-summer highlight in the veg patch that continues producing right through the winter.

overwhelming once you start looking at seed catalogues or wandering around your local nursery or garden centre in the hope of picking up ideas.

When space is an issue, the reality is that you need to be strict about what you can actually grow. Combining the main ingredients of a recipe in the same container is a nifty solution. There is also the bonus of harvesting the crops all together to make the dish and being able to invite friends and family around to enjoy them.

Most crops do well in pots – albeit in generously sized ones that give the plant plenty of reserves to continue cropping – and there are numerous dwarf or compact varieties that have been bred to thrive in a container. Herbs and salads are ideal

It is surprising how much you can grow in a small space – just plan carefully and make sure that all the varieties will be happy bedfellows.

for smaller containers and work well on windowsills and balconies too. A good rule of thumb is to stick to crops that like the same growing conditions (such as soil or compost type, amount of sunlight, temperatures) and will be ready to harvest at the same time.

However, some recipes call for herbs as well as vegetables or fruit, and this can be an issue because of the amount of water and food the different plants need. Growing herbs in their own pots within the container allows you to grow the herbs in a free-draining compost with extra grit, as well as keeping other, thirstier crops well

Straight from the container to your colander: be inspired by your freshly picked harvest of vegetables to create tasty, seasonal dishes.

watered, for example by using an upturned water bottle to direct water to their roots. Certain crops are better suited to being grown in their own pot too, such as potatoes; otherwise, their foliage may swamp the entire growing space and smother another plant trying to share the space.

Container-grown vegetables are also useful if you need to have a degree of flexibility in your garden. If the plot is small, the chances are that it will help to be able to move things about: whether to make room for a table if friends are coming around or just to keep your patio looking its best each season. Most pots are moveable – if they are very big and heavy, they can still be moved with the help of coasters – so it is easy to cope if their positions need to be changed or you want to introduce seasonal containers to maintain a year-round display. Movable containers provide a great opportunity to make the most of growing perennial tender crops, such as citrus or chives, which you could grow in containers that can be bought indoors and overwintered. Container growing also helps to restrict vigorous plants that may otherwise overpower your borders, such as mint and comfrey.

HOW TO USE THIS BOOK

THIS BOOK IS DIVIDED into two parts. The first section provides information and tips to get you off to the best start, whether you are growing crops in pots for the first time or if you could do with a bit of a refresher course.

It starts by discussing the basics, to help you plan your own growing routine and get together the plants and materials you will need: from obtaining seed or plants (see pages 14–15), choosing and positioning a container (see pages 16–17 and 23) to what equipment and compost you will need (see pages 18–21). There is even advice on using your crops (see pages 24–5) when you come to cook them.

Once you are set up, the text leads you step by step through basic techniques on sowing and planting your one-pot crops (see pages 26–31), and caring for them (see pages 32–6), to advice on when and how to harvest and store your produce (see pages 37–9).

The second and main part of the book is devoted to the pot recipes: each one designed specifically to furnish you with the produce you need to cook one of twenty-five delicious recipes – from starters to puddings. Each pot recipe gives you a plant ingredients list for one container, as well as a recipe for the dish that uses the combined produce of those plants. You will also find simple, step-by-step instructions on when to sow or plant all the plant components of the pot recipe, how to care for the plants and when to harvest them in order to make the finished dish. In addition to this, where it is appropriate, there are ideas for filling any gaps in your pots that have been created once you begin harvesting crops. All you need now is to start planting and cooking!

GROWING MONTHS are expressed as seasons rather than calendar months in the book, so that you can follow the growing season in your locality. However, in western central Europe, the seasons would translate as follows:

EARLY SPRING . . . . MARCH
MID-SPRING . . . . APRIL
LATE SPRING . . . . MAY
EARLY SUMMER . . . . . . JUNE
MIDSUMMER . . . . JULY
LATE SUMMER . . . . AUGUST
EARLY AUTUMN . . . . . . SEPTEMBER
MID-AUTUMN . . . . OCTOBER
LATE AUTUMN . . . . NOVEMBER
EARLY WINTER . . . . . . DECEMBER
MIDWINTER . . . . JANUARY
LATE WINTER . . . . FEBRUARY

Each pot recipe has an 'ingredients' list, of plants and materials

Bee-friendly plants (nectar- and/or pollen-rich) are signposted with a bee logo

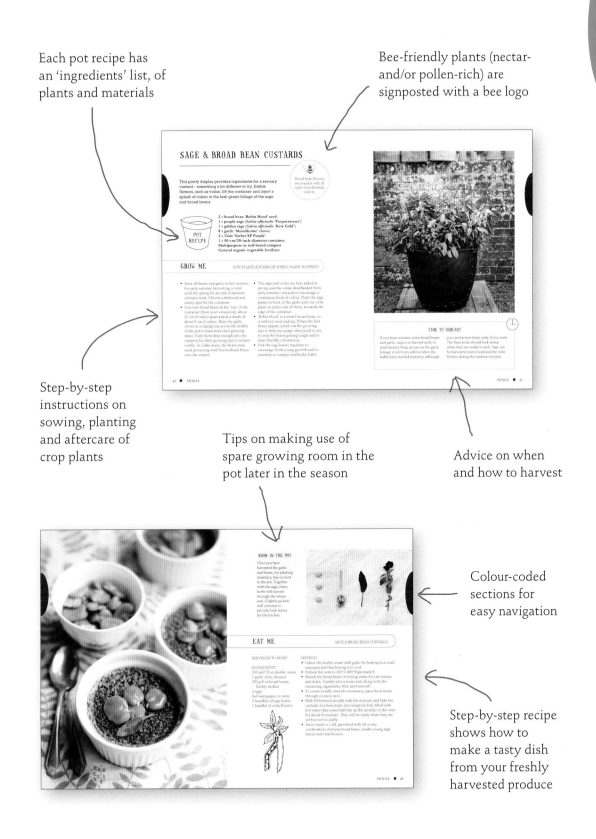

Step-by-step instructions on sowing, planting and aftercare of crop plants

Tips on making use of spare growing room in the pot later in the season

Advice on when and how to harvest

Colour-coded sections for easy navigation

Step-by-step recipe shows how to make a tasty dish from your freshly harvested produce

GETTING STARTED

THE BEST WAY TO START is to decide how many pots you can fit in your garden, balcony or roof terrace. As a general rule of thumb, fruit and vegetables need a generous-sized container, 40–50 cm/16–20 inches in diameter and as deep as possible, while some varieties will need a 1-metre/39-inch trough. Herbs can cope in slightly smaller pots. Take into account how much room there is to accommodate the eventual height and spread of a crop too: you should not cram the pots together because you need to make sure that air can flow around the pots in order to reduce the risk of pests and diseases ruining your crops.

PLANNING YOUR POTS

Once you have assessed your growing space, note whether it is in full sun or partial shade and is sheltered or exposed to the elements. It is then time to think about what you like to eat or the crops you would like to try for the first time; then you could use the recipes in this book that include some or all of those crops. Some crops will not be happy in a pot with other plants that need very different conditions, feeding or watering regimes – in the following pot recipes occasionally I have left out an ingredient, such as onion, shallot or garlic, for this reason and because it is such an easy staple to buy.

Also worth considering is when you might want to harvest your produce. If you are able to do this only at weekends or are planning a holiday, pick the recipes that will be harvestable over several weeks or will be ready before or after your trip. Tomatoes and beans can still be picked when overripe and large, because they will be fine for sauces and chutneys. However, courgettes can become less tasty marrows almost overnight if not picked when ready. Similarly, choosing to grow crops that store well, for example garlic and root vegetables, will give you more flexibility about when you can use them.

The next decision is whether you want to sow seed, buy plugs or start with young plants – you can obtain all these from garden centres, specialist nurseries, DIY stores or online suppliers. Seed is the cheapest option and, if you have space for a number of seed trays, is a great way of ensuring you have extra plants in case of mishaps or early crops failing, as well as providing a supply of free gifts for green-fingered friends and family. Another advantage of seed is the wider selection of varieties that are on offer.

However, if you are away a lot and do not have plenty of space, plugs or small plants, which can both be planted directly into the container, are a better option. Of course, you can sow seed and plant direct, to take advantage of interesting or unusual varieties as well as the more mature, 'ready-to-go', space-saving plugs.

Feel free to create your own pot recipes too, by adapting the suggestions in this book or starting from scratch. The best way to start is to make a list of your favourite fruit, vegetables and herbs – not forgetting edible flowers – and then link up produce that could grow together and be cooked together to make a particular dish. Simple combinations are a good place to start: garlic and leafy chard are happy together, like the same growing conditions and may be sown and grown to mature at the same time, ready to be transformed into a delicious pesto for a quick supper.

Think about the eventual height and spread of each crop to make sure that one does not overpower another. Courgettes work best with taller crops, such as fennel or sweetcorn, because they occupy different levels of the pot, the courgette spreading out at the base, the taller crop growing skyward.

Tempting as it might be, do not be too ambitious with your list. Crops such as onions just do not cope well in a pot with vegetables that need a lot of watering, such as sweetcorn. Bear in mind also that most crops need space to grow when you decide how many plants to use together in one pot.

Vegetables grown in containers can create eye-catching displays, so do not consign them to the bottom of the garden.

SUITABLE VARIETIES

Experiment with different varieties of your favourite type of fruit or vegetable. You will be surprised by the range of flavours.

ONE OF THE MANY JOYS of growing your own fruit, vegetables and herbs is that there is so much choice: from traditional varieties your grandad would have grown to modern F1 hybrids that promise something a little different. When it is too wet and cold to be outside during the winter months, flicking through a pile of seed catalogues in front of a roaring fire is a seasonal highlight for many gardeners. It is hard not to get carried away and in most cases gardeners' wish lists run to several pages. But that is half the fun of growing your own. The best way to whittle down your list to a manageable amount of seed is to work out your priorities. Are you looking for flavour over disease resistance? A hardy crop that ripens early if you are gardening in a cooler climate or a showstopper because of its colour or size?

If you want to use alternative varieties to those suggested in this book but still try the same recipe, check for varieties with similar qualities, such as sowing and harvesting times, bolt-resistance and hardiness. If you live in a cooler or warmer area, it is a good idea to use varieties that are more suitable for your local conditions. For example carrot 'Amsterdam Forcing 2 – Solo', climbing French bean 'Blue Lake' and pak choi 'Joi Choi' cope well with a shorter growing season and cooler temperatures, while Mediterranean herbs, sweet and chilli peppers and Swiss chard are reliable when conditions are dry and hot during a prolonged season.

It is a good idea to keep a record of the varieties you buy, making notes about them during the growing season and at harvest time. It makes it quick and easy to buy again the reliable and tasty croppers and ditch the ones that did not perform so well.

SEED TYPES

F1 seed has been bred specifically to maximize the beneficial qualities of its individual parent plants, such as good disease resistance, vigour and flavour. They are not so good if you are looking to save seed for the following season, because the seedling plants will not come 'true' (be identical to the F1 parent).

Heritage varieties have been tried and tested and handed down from generation to generation. They are open-pollinated, so will come true from seed. It is worth researching heritage varieties from your area since they will suit the climate and conditions particular to your region.

Dwarf varieties: these days there are lots of 'patio' varieties of fruit and vegetables, which have all been bred to grow and crop well in a container (see panels, below). Compact habits and smaller produce means that the plant will get everything it needs from the container (as long as it is watered and fed regularly) and will not be stressed by producing a crop in restrictive conditions. While these varieties provide an excellent place to start, container-growing does not mean that you have to limit your choices to dwarf varieties. With the right care, such as repotting the plant after a few years or reducing the size of the root ball, a lot of perennial crops will thrive in a pot too.

DWARF VEGETABLE VARIETIES

Aubergine 'Amethyst'
Aubergine 'Pinstripe'
Broad bean 'Robin Hood'
Broad bean 'The Sutton'
French bean 'Bobis d'Albenga'
French bean 'Borlotto Firetongue'
French bean (extra-fine) 'Eclarel'
French bean 'Purple Queen'
French bean 'Valdor'
Kale 'Dwarf Green Curled'
Pea (sugarsnap) 'Sugar Bon'
Pea 'Tom Thumb'
Runner bean 'Hestia'
Sweetcorn (extra-tender sweet) 'Swift'
Sweet pepper 'Mohawk'
Sweet pepper 'Redskin'
Tomato 'Red Robin'
Tomato 'Sweet 'n' Neat Scarlet'

DWARF FRUIT VARIETIES

Apple 'Bramley's Seedling'
Apple 'Flower of Kent'
Apple 'Lord Lambourne'
Apricot **Apricompakt**
Apricot 'Garden Aprigold'
Cherry 'Kordia'
Cherry 'Compact Stella'
Lemon 'Gary's Eureka'
Medlar 'Westerveld'
Nectarine 'Harko'
Peach 'Crimson Bonfire'
Peach 'Diamond'
Pear 'Garden Gem'
Pear 'Garden Pearl'
Plum 'Beauty'
Quince 'Leskovac'
Redcurrant 'Rovada'

CHOOSING A POT

SIZE AND SHAPE are important considerations when growing crops in pots. Go for the largest surface area possible because it gives you more planting space. The classic pot shape with slightly sloping sides is very suitable, particularly if you need to repot or reduce the size of the root ball of a perennial crop (fruit tree, for example) in a few years' time. A word of caution though: do not go for pots that taper too much because that design does not leave much room for roots.

In addition to practical considerations, choosing a pot you like the look of is equally important. Although perfectly practical and a useful way to recycle, nursery-style, black plastic pots are not the only option – which is good news because they are not ideal in sunny spots where they heat up so quickly, damaging the plant roots. However, they have their place if budgets are tight, if the pots are not on show or are in the shade, but there is no reason why growing crops should not be an opportunity to create a beautiful display in your garden or on your patio, balcony or roof terrace. Before you choose, consider the pros and cons of these different materials.

PLASTIC POTS
There are lots of concrete-, terracotta- and wood-effect pots made from plastic, allowing you to enjoy the best of both worlds: designer style and an attractive finish that is hard-wearing and, of course, light. It is often important to be able to move a pot, either to give the plants more sun or to overwinter them in a protected spot. However, you can always use coasters on the bottom of a pot to move it effectively.

Terracotta pots, although expensive, provide a great environment for plants because the clay breathes and draws excess moisture away from roots.

If a pot is light-coloured, it will heat up and cool down quickly, which avoids plants getting overheated in the sunniest locations. Plastic pots are easy to drill drainage holes in if needed and are durable. However, being a petroleum-based product, they have a negative impact on our environment, as they are another drain on natural resources.

METAL CONTAINERS
Especially if they are large, metal containers can heat up in the sun and make their compost dry out very quickly as well as potentially damage the plant roots. They also do not often have drainage holes, which must be drilled in the base prior to planting.

TERRACOTTA, CERAMIC AND CONCRETE POTS

Often the most stylish pots on offer, containers in these materials may have a few negative points to consider. They require more watering and maintenance because they are porous: they draw water from the soil in hot conditions, drying it out more quickly and putting plants under stress. They also retain heat, which is fine if the crops can cope with this (herbs will not mind at all), but it will damage some. This type of pot can crack in freezing conditions and they are, of course, heavy to move. They often have an inadequate number of drainage holes too. Drilling extra holes can be a frustrating business as the pots may crack or break in the process.

WOODEN CONTAINERS

This is a great material in terms of aesthetics and offers some form of insulation from the heat too. However, wooden containers need maintenance, for example staining or preserving with an eco-friendly product every season. If the container is old, such as a barrel, check it is not covered in a chemical preservative that is unsuitable for growing edible crops. Make sure that it is made from a sustainable source too.

GROWBAGS

Growbags are an inexpensive way to grow crops. In addition to the commonly available growbag, for crops such as tomatoes and peppers, there are designs made from a woven UV-resistant polypropylene, which are useful because they are strong and come in a range of sizes and colours. If space is an issue, these growbags are ideal; once you harvest the crop, you can clean and store them until the following season.

Natural materials, such as woven willow, look great with the soft leafy growth of vegetables and work well in either a traditional or modern garden.

Use coloured and textured pots to accentuate the tones of the vegetable display and create a striking feature in your garden.

USEFUL TOOLS & EQUIPMENT

ONE OF THE MANY BENEFITS of growing crops in containers is that you do not need much kit to do it. The main consideration is watering and feeding (see pages 33–4). If you do not have a lot of room for seed trays, propagators and small pots, consider buying plug plants or larger plants to plant directly into your containers. If you are growing your own, a few basic items will set you up for a season of success.

Crocks (pieces of broken terracotta or ceramic pots) or large stones: put a layer of these in the base of a container to improve drainage. Smash a few cheap terracotta pots or ask your local garden centre if they have any.

Trowel: useful for making planting holes, although you could easily use your hand. Use a trowel also to loosen any compacted soil on the surface of the pot and to remove stubborn weeds that cannot be gently pulled out.

Dibber: not essential, because a finger, pen or clean stick will do the job just as well, but if you need to give your loved ones ideas for a birthday or Christmas gift, this will do the job!

A few basic tools and items of equipment set you up perfectly for growing your own fruit and vegetables. Cane stoppers prevent eye damage as you tend your crops. Biodegradable pots, labels. twine, crocks, secateurs, vermiculite and a trowel are also useful.

Watering can: go for one as big as you can hold (when full!). The type of watering rose is important too; look for a fine rose that recreates a gentle shower of rain, rather than a gush that could displace the compost and flatten crops.

Vermiculite: use, rather than soil, to cover freshly sown seed, especially seed that needs light to germinate, such as that of lettuce; it also provides a little support to seedings as they emerge and reduces the risk of algae growing on the surface and causing the seedlings to fail.

Supports: climbing vegetables (such as beans), tall crops or plants that bear heavy fruit (such as tomatoes) will need the help of some form of support. Bamboo canes come in a range of sizes; use them either as stakes for single plants or make them into a wigwam for a group of plants, such as peas. As the plants grow, tie them in with twine or use plastic or wire ties. Pea sticks are also useful for keeping smaller plants from toppling over or holding up fruit-laden trusses. Metal and plastic obelisks are a more decorative way to prop up plants. It is always best to add any support at the time of planting, rather than wait for the plant to mature, so that you do not damage the plant roots by pushing a support into the soil when the roots have grown into it.

Labels and pens: although you will be convinced you will remember exactly what you have sown or grown in each and every pot or seed tray, it is good practice to label every one with the name (species and variety) and the date sown (use a waterproof pen). You will be surprised at how often you refer to it. Discreetly position them in the display or let the foliage naturally disguise them.

Secateurs: it is good to have a pair to hand for maintenance of your crops, whether pruning or just cleanly removing dead or diseased leaves and flowers.

Some fruit and vegetables will need staking, even if they are pot-grown. Most supports can be reused season after season.

Garden knife: ideal for cutting string, pea sticks, opening compost bags … and the list goes on.

Garden twine: use it to tie in plants to their supports.

Horticultural fleece and cloches: if you garden in a cool region or area that is prone to frosts, it is worth covering containers with fleece or individual plants with a plastic or glass cloche to avoid frost damage.

Netting: protect your crops from pests, such as birds and egg-laying cabbage white butterflies, with fine-mesh netting. Nothing is worse than finding the birds have beaten you to your fruit harvest or plants with holey, caterpillar-eaten leaves.

Gloves: by no means essential kit, but worth putting on if you are nipping into the garden before going off to work; they will save you an age spent scrubbing your nails at the sink.

WHAT COMPOST?

HERB EXPERT JEKKA MCVICAR refers to the soil as the 'engine' of a garden. In other words, make sure it is finely tuned and you will be rewarded with healthy, productive plants. It is a great way to think about the growing medium you choose to use in your pots. Do not be tempted to use garden soil on its own, because it does not contain the balance of nutrients needed for specific crops nor provide enough air or drainage; these are key for container-grown crops. It is also likely to contain weed seeds and even pests and diseases. It is best to go for a specifically designed compost for containers, which has good drainage and aeration and has been sterilized.

The key to success with growing your own is the compost you use. Peat free and organic is by far the best choice.

TYPES OF COMPOST

There is a wide range of composts available to suit your growing needs. They are easy to find in your local garden centre, specialist nursery or DIY store and online.

Soilless compost: specially created for containers and made from any combination of materials, such as peat, coir fibre, bark or vermiculite, depending on what use it will be put to – seed or cuttings, small container plants, such as hanging baskets, or larger containers needing very good drainage. Soilless compost offers good drainage, aeration and a neutral pH. It is also light and in general provides enough nutrients for about the first six weeks, requiring you to add fertilizer thereafter.

Soil-based compost: often called John Innes compost, which refers to the horticultural institute set up in 1904 to create an optimum growing medium for plants. This type of compost contains soil that has been heat-treated to reduce contamination by plant diseases. It contains a mixture of soil (for bulk), clay (which stores and releases nutrients), sphagnum-moss peat (for water retention and aeration), sand (for drainage) and additional nutrients including nitrogen, phosphates and potassium. Use it for woody crops (such as fruit trees) or plants that need deep, rich soil (such as potatoes).

Peat-free compost: if you are not keen on using peat-based composts (some of us believe harvesting peat from lowland bogs has a negative effect on the environment as well as on the wildlife that depends on these habitats), there are plenty of alternatives on offer. You do need to treat peat-free compost differently, because it dries out more easily. Read the label and go for brands that provide plenty of information about how to use and care for the product. Look out for composts that have beneficial additives like biochar, seaweed and mycorrhizal fungi, because these all help container-grown crops.

Ericaceous compost: crops such as blueberries and cranberries need an acid soil, with a pH level between four and five (a neutral soil is pH7; alkaline soils have a pH above seven). Ericaceous compost provides the right acidity for these crops.

USING COMPOST

Some crops, especially Mediterranean herbs, need a very open, free-draining growing medium. You can improve proprietary general composts to provide the right conditions by adding horticultural grit (which has been sterilized), or perlite, which improves aeration and prevents the compost from becoming waterlogged and compacted. Work in ratios such as 3:1 of compost:horticultural grit.

It is best to use fresh compost each year if you are completely replanting a pot with new crops, but with large containers you could remove only the top two-thirds of compost and replace it with new compost each spring. Topdressing (scraping off the top 7–10 cm/3–4 inches of old compost and refreshing with new compost) each year is sufficient for perennial crops that are staying in the same container until they need repotting (after three or four years of growth).

Add in horticultural grit or perlite to compost to change its structure, creating extra drainage and making it lighter.

HOW MUCH COMPOST FILLS A POT?

Use this table as a guide as to how much compost you will need to fill each container.

POT SIZE (DIAMETER X DEPTH)	VOLUME OF COMPOST
20 × 20 cm/8 × 8 inches	6 litres
30 × 20 cm/12 × 8 inches	12 litres
30 × 30 cm/12 × 12 inches	24 litres
40 × 20 cm/16 × 8 inches	24 litres
40 × 30 cm/16 × 12 inches	36 litres
40 × 40 cm/16 × 16 inches	48 litres
50 × 20 cm/20 × 8 inches	42 litres
50 × 30 cm/20 × 12 inches	60 litres
50 × 40 cm/20 × 16 inches	78 litres
50 × 50 cm/20 × 20 inches	96 litres
1-metre-long × 50-cm-wide/40 × 20 inch trough	390 litres

POSITIONING THE POT

IN THE MAIN, CROPS PREFER plenty of sun – about six to eight hours if possible – but do bear in mind that, if in direct sun all day, they dry out quickly and need regular watering to compensate. It is a good idea to provide a bit of shelter if possible for these sun-loving crops. A wall, shed or hedge will provide some respite from harsher conditions, such as wind, which can dry out the pots and damage the crops, as well as rain, which if heavy and prolonged results in the containers becoming waterlogged and the crops being battered. Crops like beans, peas, aubergines and peppers especially benefit from protection in windy, exposed sites. Some crops cope with shade and some positively thrive – currants, gooseberries, lettuce, radicchio, peas and spinach are perfect for this difficult growing spot.

In cool regions, crops appreciate some protection against frost and falling temperatures; horticultural fleece or cloches help. Monitor the changing conditions and wrap or cover crops accordingly. Crops that continue to provide a harvest over winter may also require similar protection or need to be moved into a greenhouse or shed.

Using pot feet helps excess water to drain away from the container and prevent the roots from sitting in sodden compost.

Paving or gravel is a good surface on which to stand your container. Terracotta pot feet, which lift the container off the ground, help the pot to drain properly and reduce the risk of it sitting in a puddle of water or of pests entering from underneath. Leave plenty of room between your pots to allow the air to circulate and reduce the risk of pests and diseases spreading from one to the other. Consider the size of each container too, positioning the taller ones behind the shorter ones to avoid them blocking out the light.

Finding a spot for containers close to the house is ideal, so that you can watch out for pests and diseases, keep them well watered, and most of all, harvest them easily. After all your work on growing your crops, you do not want to miss picking them when they are at their ripest.

Exploit backdrops to accentuate your pot display, if possible: plain walls are often best, allowing the shapes, colours and textures of the container and its crops to stand out. Arrange groups of containers to act as a screen or to create a temporary 'hedge' in the garden.

Some varieties of fruit, vegetables and herbs are perennial and can overwinter, but you may need to protect them from severe spells of cold by covering them with horticultural fleece.

SERVING SUGGESTIONS

SOME OF THE CROPS FEATURED in the pot recipes in this book will produce more crops than you need to make a specific dish, while others will provide just a couple of servings. The yield also will vary from plant to plant and variety to variety. For many of the featured crops, you can use the produce as and when it is ready and still have enough ingredients for the dish.

Courgettes for example provide a bounty nearly all summer long, so do not wait until the rest of the crops in the pot are ready – enjoy picking and using your fresh, home-grown cucurbits!

Beetroots may be used as baby vegetables – a delicious raw addition to a salad – while a more mature, larger root is perfect for making the soup. Similarly, young and tender **chard** and **carrots** are delicious eaten raw and in salads, when left to mature, the larger crops go a little farther and are ideal for making a pesto.

Herbs are really good value: they are ready to harvest from early summer and provide fresh pickings right up until autumn; in many cases, as with thyme, parsley and rosemary, they overwinter too.

You can choose to harvest many crops before they mature to serve as baby vegetables and tender baby leaves. **Garlic**, **shallots** and **onions** reach maturity and are ready for harvest when their leaves turn yellow and topple over; however, there is nothing to stop you picking them as baby vegetables, earlier in the season. 'Wet' or young garlic is delicious and is valued for its softer, more delicate flavour.

You can treat many **leafy vegetables** as cut-and-come-again salad crops by picking the young leaves regularly over a period of

Courgette flowers are edible, delicious and highly ornamental and make this much-undervalued crop well worth growing.

time. Brassicas, such as **cabbage**, may be cropped twice if you are prepared to have a smaller initial crop. Score an 'X' on the cut-down stem after the first picking, to encourage fresh new growth and a second crop of leaves.

Many of the plants featured in these pot recipes provide other edible treats, as well as the primary fruit or vegetable crop required in the dish. **Fennel** pollen is much sought after as an ingredient by professional chefs to garnish fish, while the dried seed livens up many soups and stews.

Young **beetroot leaves** are delicious in salads and **courgette flowers** stuffed or

Do not forget that edible flowers provide welcome interest to container displays and are colourful, tasty garnishes for a recipe too.

Dry your surplus chillies: it is easy to do and they make a welcome addition to pep up soups and stews during the winter months.

covered in a tempura batter and deep-fried are wonderful delicacies that are hard to find in the shops.

Do not despair if your **salad crops** bolt and start to flower – while this might mean the leaves are too bitter to use, their delicate, colourful flowers look gorgeous sparingly sprinkled over a dish and many of them are tasty too. In the main, it is best to remove the flower stalk, pistils and anthers and use just the petals to garnish a dish. Take care to check that you have identified the flower correctly and that it is edible, because some flowers are poisonous to eat, such as those of the foxglove (*Digitalis*).

If your **tomatoes** have not ripened by the end of the season, pick all the green fruits and bring them indoors; place them with other fully ripe tomatoes on a sunny windowsill or with a banana in a paper bag to speed up the ripening process. Alternatively, transform them into a delectable green chutney or fry them as a vegetable. You can use green (unripe) **chillies** for a milder flavour or, if you prefer more of a kick, leave them to ripen fully and change colour. Pick and dry surplus chillies by stringing them up and leaving them in a warm, dry place, so you can use them in dishes over the winter months.

SEEDS & SOWING

SOWING SEED IS MUCH CHEAPER than buying plugs or plants and it is hard to beat that sense of satisfaction when the seeds germinate and emerge through the compost and, some weeks later, you are able to plant out home-grown young plants.

Depending on the amount of seed you are sowing, choose a 9-cm/3½-inch pot, a seed tray or a modular tray. Many pot recipes in this book call for a packet of seed, but you do not have to sow the entire packet – use your discretion. If the pot recipe calls for three plants from a packet of seed, sow double the amount of seed as plants required as an insurance and use a 9-cm/3½-inch pot or three cells of a modular tray, with two seeds sown in each individual cell. Feel free to sow more if you have space and can plant the seedlings in other containers or other parts of the garden. You may even want to grow extra plants to give to fellow home-growing enthusiasts.

Whichever type of tray or pot you use, always fill it with seed compost and drop the tray or pot on to a table to knock out any air. If needed, add a little more compost to reach just under the rim of the tray or pot and firm well. Use an empty pot or tray of the same size or a 'tamper' tool to do this – the aim is to create a firm, flat surface upon which to sow the seed. Use a watering can with a fine rose to water the compost and allow to drain: it is better to do this before you sow the seed to avoid displacing it with the force of the water.

Mix fine seed with fine sand to help spread the seed evenly and sow it on the surface of the compost. Then use a layer of

STEP BY STEP: SOWING SEED

1

Fill a seed tray with seed compost to just under the rim. Firm down with another, same-sized tray.

2

Water the compost before sowing seed. Sow each type of seed as directed on the packet.

3

Cover smaller, delicate seed with vermiculite rather than compost to reduce the risk of damping off.

STEP BY STEP: PRICKING OUT

1. Fill a 9-cm/3½-inch pot with compost to just under the rim, firm and make a hole in the centre.

2. Carefully lift a seedling, gathering the soil around its delicate roots, and transplant into the pot.

3. Space the roots out in the hole. Firm the compost gently around the seedling and water well.

vermiculite, rather than compost, to cover it. Vermiculite is lighter and allows light through it – most fine seed needs light to germinate – and it also provides a bit of support as the seed germinates and the vulnerable seedlings emerge.

To sow seed at a certain depth, as directed on the seed packet, it is best to sow on the compost surface and then cover it with the right amount of compost. Make sure you leave enough room at the top of the pot or tray to accommodate this layer when you initially fill it with compost. For larger seed, such as that of beans and pumpkins, make a planting hole with a pen or your finger to the appropriate depth, drop one seed in and cover with compost.

CARE OF SEEDLINGS⸮

The ideal place for most seeds to germinate is in a dry, warm environment: a greenhouse or potting-shed bench is perfect, but a sunny windowsill will do just as well. Cover your tray or pot with a plastic bag propped up with a short cane, to keep in the moisture. Some

seed may require a heat source to trigger germination, in which case use a heated propagator with a lid.

Do not let the compost dry out, but make sure it is not waterlogged, because wet compost will cause the seedlings to be vulnerable to issues such as damping off. This is caused by several soil-borne fungi, often the culprits when seedlings fail to emerge or completely collapse. Avoid damping off by making sure that all your pots and trays are clean before use; also sow seed thinly to avoid overcrowding and ensure that there is plenty of air circulating around emerging seedlings. Once seedlings are infected, there is no remedy: dispose of the seed tray, compost and seedlings and sow fresh seed in a clean tray or pot.

Once tray-sown seedlings are large enough to handle, prick them out into 9-cm/3½-inch pots to grow on prior to planting in their final positions. For each seedling, hold one of the leaves rather than the tender stem and use a dibber to ease out the roots from the compost, then gently plant it into its new pot.

PLANTING PLUGS
& CONTAINER-GROWN PLANTS

TO PREPARE YOUR CONTAINER for planting your pot-recipe crops, make sure that the container has a sufficient amount of drainage holes for the size of the pot – as a rule of thumb, you need six to eight 1-cm/½-inch holes in the bottom of a 35-cm/14-inch container. If the container has just one drainage hole in the base and is made from a material that can be drilled without cracking, drill a few more evenly spaced holes.

Add a layer of crocks (terracotta pot shards) to help any excess water drain through the drainage holes and then fill with the appropriate compost. If the plants in the pot recipe require a free-draining soil, now is the time to add horticultural grit or perlite to the compost. For example, to achieve a very free-draining soil beloved by herbs such as thyme and oregano, mix 50:50 grit and compost.

Use an appropriate amount of organic fertilizer for the size of the pot, as directed by the manufacturer. Add half the amount when the container is about half-filled with compost and mix it in well. Add the remaining compost and then sprinkle on the remaining amount of fertilizer, mixing it in well again. Fill the container to at least 2.5 cm/1 inch below the rim, to prevent the compost from washing over the sides when you water it.

WHAT SIZE PLANT?

Plugs are seedling plants that are sold in small plugs of compost, rather than in containers. Mini plugs are sent out in early spring; the standard plugs, which are a little larger, arrive later in spring. These seedling plants need to be potted on immediately

ABOVE Tease apart dense clumps of seedlings and prick them out individually into 9-cm/3½-inch pots to grow on, before planting them in the final container. RIGHT It is a good idea to grow additional seedlings in small pots so you can fill any gaps in the container that appear after harvesting the main crop.

into 9-cm/3½-inch pots and left to grow for a month or two in order to develop a strong root system.

As with plugs, it is a good idea to wait until the risk of frosts has passed to plant your home-grown seedling plants and small container-grown, garden-ready plants into 9-cm/3½-inch pots.

Unless otherwise stated (see pages 40–137), a 9-cm/3½-inch pot is an ideal size of starter pot for many of the crops that feature in the recipes. With some herbs

When the seedlings are large enough to handle, and the risk of frost has passed, you can plant them directly into the final container, keeping their plugs of compost intact to avoid any check to their growth.

(such as bay) and fruits (such as redcurrants) go for a 1-litre/13-cm or larger-sized pot to overcome the issue of their slower growth rate and to guarantee that the plants are sufficiently mature to crop in the first season. You could plant container-grown crops all year round, but it is best to plant from autumn to spring, when the plant is dormant or breaking into growth.

Some crops are supplied as bare-root plants (at least one-year-old field-grown plants, with bare roots packed in compost or plastic). Crops such as blackberry and raspberry canes and redcurrant bushes are available bare-rooted in autumn to late winter. You should plant bare-root crops as soon as possible once they arrive, but if it is too cold or wet either pot them up or heel them in (cover the roots in a temporary trench outdoors).

PLANTING CROPS IN YOUR CONTAINER

Whether the plant is large or small, the technique is similar. Water each plant well immediately before planting. Make the planting hole as deep and a little wider

STEP BY STEP: PLANTING PLUGS

1 Gently remove each plug by pushing a finger through the base of the cell to pop it out.

2 Make a hole about the same size as the plug with a trowel. Plant the plug and firm it in gently.

3 Water well. Thin growing seedlings as required, by removing the weakest or harvesting baby crops.

than the pot it is growing in. Carefully remove the pot so as not to damage the root system. Place the plant in the planting hole and check that its root ball is at the same level in the new container as it was in its tray or pot. Backfill with compost, firm the soil around the stem and water it in well, even if it is raining.

If planting canes or bare-root plants, soak the roots in a bucket of water before planting. Make the hole large enough to allow the roots to spread out and check that the soil mark at the base of the stem sits at the compost surface. Hold the stem at the correct level as you backfill the hole, teasing the compost between the roots as you go.

STEP BY STEP: PLANTING UP YOUR CONTAINER

Make sure that the container has enough drainage holes. Cover the base with a layer of crocks.

Fill with compost to about 5 cm/ 2 inches below the rim. Add some slow-release organic fertilizer.

Make each hole a little wider and deeper than the plant's root ball. Add horticultural grit if needed.

Tease out the plant roots and place in the hole at the level it was in its pot. Backfill and firm gently.

Once the container is planted up, water well – and keep watered as the plants establish.

Check the container regularly for pests and diseases. Act promptly at the first sign of any problem.

WATERING

UNLIKE CROPS GROWN in the ground, container-grown plants cannot send down their roots to a natural water source. Even a good shower of rain will not always give your crops a good drink, because their leaves may be too dense to let enough water through. To make sure that your pots do not dry out and stress your crops, water regularly. In hot weather, depending on the crop and the pot size, you may need to water twice a day. Small pots dry out more quickly than larger ones, which need a long soak at regular intervals. Unless the crop is very thirsty (tomatoes and sweetcorn), large pots should not need daily attention, but always check that the compost is not dry.

Too much watering could also affect plants adversely, causing leaves to wilt or brown or even die. The best way to avoid overwatering is to make sure that the pot has sufficient drainage (holes and crocks). Before watering, test the soil with your finger: if it feels wet it does not require watering. Some plants may need more water than others in the same container – insert a cut-off, plastic bottle near the roots of the thirstier plants to direct the water to their roots, rather than all the surrounding compost in the container.

KEEPING THE COMPOST MOIST

Watering can: this is ideal for watering containers. Take the rose off, because it is easier and more effective if you direct a steady flow of water to the roots rather than spraying the foliage, which may be

If you cannot check and water your pots daily, it is worth thinking about alternatives like water-retaining granules, watering systems or mulch.

damaged. It is also important if you want to avoid fungal diseases like mildew on crops such as onions, garlic, courgettes and soft fruits.

Water-retaining granules: opinion is divided as to their effectiveness, but if you are often away for weekends they are worth incorporating into the compost at planting time to reduce the amount of watering required. However, they are not a substitute for proper watering.

Mulching: while mulching is a useful way to suppress weeds, keep roots cool and retain moisture, most crops in containers do this naturally by shading the compost with their foliage. However, apply a mulch when the compost surface is exposed, for example when crops are young, or if you are growing a fruit tree or standard bay or lavender in a container. Crushed shells look pretty and go some way to deter slugs and snails.

Watering systems: leaky hoses and automatic droppers are easy to install and do not cost the earth. They are essential if you are not at home every day and cannot rely on a neighbour to water your pots.

LEFT A good-sized watering can, with a fine rose, is essential for container gardening; it is important to make sure that pots do not dry out.

FEEDING

PLANTS IN CONTAINERS rely entirely on nutrients and trace elements being added regularly to the compost, to give them everything they need to grow and produce a crop, whereas crops that are planted in the ground can draw on the natural elements found in the soil.

A good option is to mix a slow-release organic fertilizer (includes 'hoof and horn' and bonemeal) into the container compost at planting time to release nutrients slowly for steady growth and a high-quality crop. Follow the manufacturer's guidelines on the correct amount to use with the specific volume of compost in each container. The slow-release feed is a great boost for the initial growing period, of about six weeks, but you need to top it up with an organic liquid feed: add it to the containers from mid-spring to late summer. Make sure the soil is moist whenever you apply liquid fertilizer to the pot, to help the roots absorb the nutrients more quickly.

THE THREE MAIN NUTRIENTS

Look for the N:P:K ratio on the product packaging, because it indicates the relative ratios in the feed of nitrogen (N) for leafy growth, phosphorus (P) for healthy roots and shoots and potassium (K) or potash for flowers and fruits. For example chicken manure pellets have a ratio of 4.3:3.2:3.2, so are slightly higher in nitrogen, whereas a seaweed feed (5:2:5) and blood, fish and bone (5:3:5) have balanced levels of both nitrogen and potassium so are more general fertilizers.

FRUITING AND LEAFY CROPS

If you are growing fruiting crops, look for a higher ratio of potassium (K), such as 4:3:8, whereas leafy crops, such as spinach and beet, need a higher ratio of nitrogen (N), such as 25:15:15. You might need to feed crops differently at different times in the growing season, for example with a general or high-nitrogen fertilizer for leafy growth while plants are young, then with a high-potash fertilizer when they are coming into bud, flower and fruit. If you prefer to use a balanced, general fertilizer all year round, go for a ratio of 20:20:20, but you may not get the maximum yield from every crop.

RIGHT Container-grown plants should be fed regularly during the growing season to provide the nutrients they need.
FAR RIGHT After about six weeks, top up the slow-release organic fertilizer with a two-weekly application of liquid feed.

CULTIVATING YOUR CROPS

THE LEVEL OF CARE REQUIRED to maintain your container is governed by the specific needs of the crops in it. It is important to keep the pot tidy and clear away dead or diseased leaves and flowers regularly. Check underneath sprawling crops, such as courgette and cabbages, removing old or damaged leaves.

Support crops such as tomatoes, beans and peas with canes and tie in the stems as the plants grow. Use a cane that will be taller than the mature plant, for example 90–125 cm/3–4 ft for dwarf varieties, 1.75–2.5 m/6–8 ft for tomatoes and beans. Canes are available in a range of materials, including bamboo, hazel, coated steel and plastic. Carefully tie plants into the support with string or twine: wind it around the support and knot it first, then loosely tie around the stem and knot again. Alternatively, use flexible plastic or a foam-coated metal ties. Insert stakes at planting, rather than risk damaging the roots later.

Pinch out side shoots or growing tips of crops such as tomatoes, beans, peppers and peas to control their shape and final heights. Pick herbs and deadhead flowering plants, such as marigolds and violas, regularly to keep them compact and bushy and to produce an ongoing supply of young leaves or edible flowers. Remove strawberry runners to focus energy on fruit production and mulch with straw to keep the fruits clean. Prune or train fruit trees according to the season, for a good crop in the following year and for a healthy, strong, open habit.

To encourage abundant crops, position pots of nectar- or pollen-rich flowers next to your crops to attract bees and other pollinating insects. Go for plants such as lavenders, alliums, catmints (*Nepeta*), foxgloves (*Digitalis*), hardy geraniums, verbascums, *Verbena bonariensis* and penstemons.

Protect your containers if temperatures drop. Cover the vulnerable crop or entire pot with a cloche, horticultural fleece or bubble wrap. Avoid the material resting on the crop, which encourages pests and disease through lack of ventilation. The fleece or bubble wrap should be 7–10 cm/3–4 inches above the crop: drape it over canes (one in each corner of the pot, to create a frame). In severe cold or to overwinter, move pots into the shelter of a greenhouse, conservatory or outhouse.

FAR LEFT Carefully tie in stems with twine, using a figure-of-eight to prevent the cane and stem rubbing together.
LEFT To encourage tomato plants to grow upwards and stop them becoming too bushy, pinch out the side shoots.

PESTS & DISEASES

CROPS IN CONTAINERS ARE just as susceptible as those in the ground to attack from pests and diseases. However, containers are easier to keep an eye on if in close proximity to the house, allowing you to take swift action at the first sign of infection. Here is a rogue's gallery of the most common problems you are likely to face.

Slugs and snails: obvious culprits, being drawn to young, leafy foliage. While pellets and copper tape are worth a try, you really cannot beat making regular torch-lit expeditions in the evenings to remove and dispose of them one by one.

Vine weevils: a problem for container-grown crops, because the adult beetles munch tell-tale notches out of leaves in the growing season and the white grubs lay waste to the roots in autumn and winter, causing the plant to wilt. Strawberries are particularly susceptible. A chemical drench is available for ornamental plants but is unsuitable for edible crops, so a biological control is the best course of action. Use a nematode, either *Steinernema kraussei* or *Heterorhabditis megidis*, but follow the instructions carefully because they need particular conditions to work well. An evening, torch-lit hunt for adult beetles is also recommended.

Aphids: green- and blackfly are the most likely aphids to attack broad beans and other crops. Squash them with your fingers, hose them off or spray with an organic insecticide to eradicate the problem.

Cabbage white caterpillars: this pest can cause havoc on brassicas, such as cabbage or pak choi, but it is not just this pest that creates huge holes in your crops. Regularly check the undersides of

Companion plants, such as marigolds, offer a clever way to entice pests away from your precious vegetable plants and protect your crop.

vulnerable leaves and remove eggs or young caterpillars by hand to keep on top of the problem. Resort to a contact insecticide for bigger infestations.

Algae, liverworts and mosses: these develop on the compost surface if it is compacted or waterlogged. Simply topdress with fresh compost and try adding an ornamental mulch, such as gravel or small pebbles.

HELP IS AT HAND
Companion plants may help to keep some pests at bay and can introduce colour and interest to the container. However, they are a luxury if space is tight in the crop pot. Try positioning separate pots of companion plants next to the main cropping container. The strong scent of French marigolds is great for attracting away carrot fly and confusing whitefly, deterring them from visiting tomatoes. Nasturtiums offer an alternative breeding ground for cabbage-white caterpillars, instead of the more precious cabbage, kale and cauliflower crops, as well as luring aphids away from French and runner beans.

HARVESTING & STORAGE

CHEFS ADVOCATE HARVESTING crops at different times throughout the season, because baby vegetables have quite a different texture and taste to more mature ones. While it is tempting to wait for crops to reach the size of shop-bought ones, bear in mind that home-grown vegetables, and especially container-grown varieties, might not bulk up in the same way. Remember, as you reap the benefits of all your hard work, that you are looking for flavour and texture over size when it comes to picking produce.

HARVESTING PRODUCE

As a rule of thumb, harvesting any crop is best done in the early morning, after the dew has evaporated, or on cloudy days, because the crops will have a higher water content; of course, this might not always be practical. Before you start picking, make sure that you have a colander, bucket or basket to collect your crops.

Some crops are best harvested using a knife, secateurs or scissors, for example asparagus, tomatoes, leafy crops and herbs, but in the main you do not need many tools. Twist individual tomatoes from the vine, pinch off beans and peas with your fingernails and gently rock courgettes up and down to separate them from the parent plant. Of course, the benefit of growing crops in containers also means ripe and ready produce is easy to reach without needing ladders and other paraphernalia.

While it is good practice to pick herbs regularly to encourage fresh growth and good plant health, if the plant is good for bees and other pollinating insects, why not let a few stems flower to help out the wildlife a little. If you prefer to crop

Fully mature crops are delicious, but chefs recommend trying vegetables when they are small 'baby veg' to enjoy the flavour at its most intense.

everything and prevent plants from going to seed, that is fine.

In a perfect world, you would harvest the exact amount of produce you need to create a dish the same day – indeed, this book shows you how to do it. Most of the following pot recipes require most or all of the crops produced by the pots in order to make the dish. This is great if storage is an issue and you do not relish the thought of eating a particular vegetable night after night. That said, some crops just keep on

Plait garlic stems together to store the bulbs until you want to use them. It is easier than it looks and the finished result is rather lovely.

giving – courgettes and tomatoes spring to mind – and it pays to think about how to store excess produce if you are not going to give it away to friends and family.

STORING YOUR HARVEST

Some crops such as tomatoes, chillis and sweet peppers are fine left on the plant to ripen or picked and left in the kitchen to change colour. However, it is useful to have a cool, dry place to store produce such as onions, garlic and shallots, as well as root vegetables and tree fruits, so you can use them as and when required. A garage is ideal, but an unheated cupboard under the stairs is fine too. Store the crops appropriately: individually wrap tree fruits, such as apples and pears, in newspaper and lay them in a box without touching, to prevent rotting. Dry onions and garlics properly before storing, either plaited or laid out in rows in a box. You could store carrots and beetroot in a bucket of dry sand, otherwise known as a 'clamp'.

You might also want to consider other ways to preserve your bounty, ready to enjoy at a time when fresh crops are not so abundant. Preserving is an excellent way to store produce. Jams, pickles and chutneys are easy and satisfying to make, but they really come into their own during leaner months, adding vibrancy to home-cooked dishes. Get together with friends and swap produce to make different preserves or hand over finished jars in return for some of theirs. Lots of vegetables, fruit and herbs freeze really well and it is a great way of locking in flavour and nutrients.

RIGHT Preserve gluts of crops, ready to open and enjoy during the winter months when there is not much in the way of fresh home-grown produce.

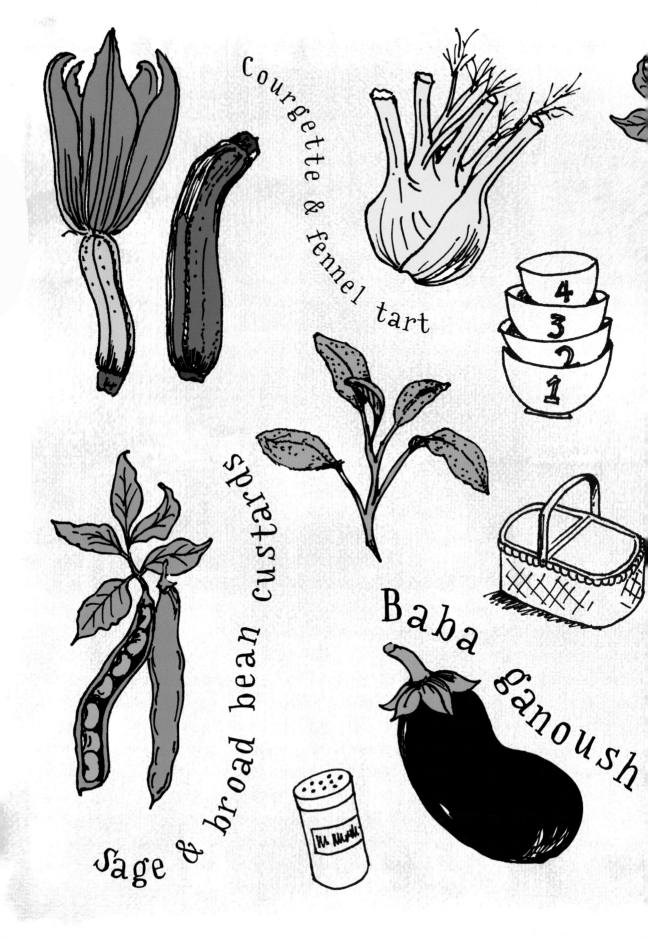

Courgette & fennel tart

4
3
2
1

Sage & broad bean custards

Baba ganoush

Hummus three ways

PICNICS

Honey & thyme blackberries with thyme shortbreads

COURGETTE & FENNEL TART

Courgettes are a must for the patio vegetable garden. They provide a welcome flash of colour, with their sunny yellow flowers that are followed by a tasty and truly versatile crop (you can eat them raw, stir-fried, pickled or roasted). If you pick them often, you will have a steady harvest all summer long. Teaming this crop with tall, frondy fennel gives this display height and structure, not to mention a delicious flavour combination in the finished dish.

POT RECIPE

5 x Florence fennel 'Sirio' seed
1 x courgette 'Piccolo' F1 seed
5 x onion 'Forum' sets
1 x pot marigold (*Calendula officinalis* 'Indian Prince')
1 x 50-cm/20-inch-diameter container
Multipurpose or soil-based compost
General organic vegetable fertilizer

GROW ME

PLANT IN EARLY SPRING; SOW IN MID-SPRING

- Place the container in a sunny, sheltered position and fill it with compost, mixing in the granular organic fertilizer, to release nutrients slowly for steady growth and a high-quality crop.
- If planting onions in rows in the ground you would aim to space them 10 cm/4 inches apart, but they can be a bit cosier in containers if you are not fussy about harvesting slightly smaller – but equally tasty – bulbs. The trick is to harvest one or two bulbs early, allowing the remaining few bulbs to mature to full size. In early spring, plant the sets in a group to one side of the container. Make sure that their tips are just poking out above the surface of the compost.

- Wait until mid-spring to start off the fennel, courgettes and pot marigolds indoors, in modular trays. Sow courgettes one seed per cell, pot marigolds two seeds per cell and fennel seeds around three per cell; thin when about 5 cm/2 inches tall to one seedling per cell. Plant the seedlings out into the container when all risk of frost has passed in late spring – look for signs of the roots at the bases of the trays as an indication that they are ready for their final position.
- Keep well watered and feed every two weeks. Cover half the depth of the fennel bulb with more compost when it starts to swell. Keep picking the pot marigolds to prolong flowering.

TIME TO HARVEST

By the time the fennel is ready for harvest, 14–16 weeks after sowing in late summer, you will be able to lift the onions too, as their foliage will be turning brown by then. This compact variety of courgette will most likely give you more courgettes than you might need for this dish. Feel free to pick the fruits even if you are not ready to make the tart because this will stop the fruits getting too large and will provide you with a continuous supply of produce. Pick the pot marigold flowers just before serving your tart.

EAT ME

SERVES FOUR

INGREDIENTS
3 courgettes, thinly sliced
1 fennel bulb, the hard core
    removed, thinly sliced
1 onion, thinly sliced
Splash of olive oil
Salt and pepper, to taste
Small handful of
    chopped parsley
1 × 500-g/18-oz pack
    puff pastry
100 g/3½ oz mature cheddar,
    grated
1 handful of marigold petals

METHOD
- Preheat the oven to 200°C/400°F/gas mark 6.
- Put the courgettes, fennel, onion, oil, salt and pepper in a roasting tin and toss until evenly coated. Cover with aluminium foil and roast for 30 minutes. Remove and leave to cool.
- Drain excess juice from the vegetables and mix in the parsley.
- Roll out the puff pastry, to about 20 x 30 cm/8 x 12 inches and lay on a baking sheet. Score a line about 2.5 cm/1 inch from the edge without cutting all the way through.
- Scatter the roasted vegetables over the pastry and cover with cheese.
- Bake for 20 minutes until the pastry has risen and browned.
- Remove and serve hot or cold. Scatter the marigold petals over the finished dish for a splash of home-grown colour.

ROOM IN THE POT

Sow cut-and-come-
again salad leaves
as you harvest each
fennel, to serve as a
garnish with the next
tart you make.

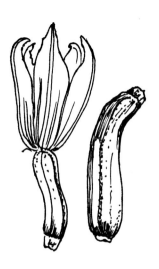

SAGE & BROAD BEAN CUSTARDS

This pretty display provides ingredients for a savoury custard – something a bit different to try. Edible flowers, such as violas, lift the container and inject a splash of colour to the lush green foliage of the sage and broad beans.

Broad bean flowers are popular with all types of pollinating insects.

POT RECIPE

2 x broad bean 'Robin Hood' seed
1 x purple sage (*Salvia officinalis* 'Purpurascens')
1 x golden sage (*Salvia officinalis* 'Kew Gold')
8 x garlic 'Messidrome' cloves
2 x *Viola* 'Sorbet XP Purple'
1 x 50-cm/20-inch-diameter container
Multipurpose or soil-based compost
General organic vegetable fertilizer

GROW ME

SOW IN LATE AUTUMN OR SPRING; PLANT IN SPRING

- Start off beans and garlic in late autumn for early summer harvesting or wait until the spring for an end-of-summer culinary treat. Choose a sheltered and sunny spot for the container.
- Sow two broad beans at the 'top' of the container (from your viewpoint), about 20 cm/8 inches apart and at a depth of about 5 cm/2 inches. Plant the garlic cloves in a zigzag line across the middle of the pot to maximize their growing space. Push them deep enough into the compost for their growing tips to remain visible. In colder areas, the beans may need protecting with horticultural fleece over the winter.

- The sage and violas are best added in spring, and the violas deadheaded from early summer onwards to encourage a continuous flush of colour. Plant the sage plants in front of the garlic and one viola plant on either side of them, towards the edge of the container.
- 'Robin Hood' is a dwarf broad bean, so it will not need staking. When the first beans appear, pinch out the growing tips to help encourage other pods to set, to stop the beans getting tough and to deter blackfly infestations.
- Pick the sage leaves regularly to encourage fresh young growth and to maintain a compact and bushy habit.

TIME TO HARVEST

If you have autumn-sown broad beans and garlic, expect to harvest early to midsummer. Keep an eye on the garlic foliage: it will turn yellow when the bulbs have reached maturity, although you can harvest them early if you want. The bean pods should look plump when they are ready to pick. Sage can be harvested year-round and the viola flowers during the summer months.

ROOM IN THE POT

Once you have harvested the garlic and beans, try planting rosemary, bay or mint in the pot. Together with the sage, these herbs will survive through the winter and, if lightly picked, will continue to provide fresh leaves for the kitchen.

EAT ME

SAGE & BROAD BEAN CUSTARDS

SERVES SIX TO EIGHT

INGREDIENTS
200 ml/7 fl oz double cream
1 garlic clove, bruised
250 g/9 oz broad beans,
    freshly shelled
2 eggs
Salt and pepper, to taste
2 handfuls of sage leaves
1 handful of viola flowers

METHOD
- Infuse the double cream with garlic by heating in a small saucepan and then leaving it to cool.
- Preheat the oven to 200°C/400°F/gas mark 6.
- Blanch the broad beans in boiling water for one minute and drain. Transfer into a mixer and, along with the remaining ingredients, blitz until smooth.
- To create a really smooth consistency, pass the mixture through a coarse sieve.
- Half-fill buttered moulds with the mixture and bake the custards in a bain-marie (an ovenproof dish, filled with hot water that comes halfway up the moulds) in the oven for about 30 minutes. They will be ready when they are set but not too puffy.
- Serve warm or cold, garnished with all or any combination of plump broad beans, tender young sage leaves and viola flowers.

HUMMUS THREE WAYS

Impress your friends with deliciously different types of hummus. Broad beans, carrot and beetroot make colourful, nutritious and delicious alternatives to the traditional dish. The broad bean variation has no chickpeas so perhaps it is more of a dip! Either way, they are all easy to make and are perfect seasonal treats. These vegetables are easy to grow too; the beetroot variety is bolt-resistant so it can be sown early.

Broad bean flowers will attract bees, butterflies and other pollinating insects.

POT RECIPE

1 x packet of broad bean 'The Sutton' seed
1 x packet of carrot 'Caracas' seed
1 x packet of beetroot 'Moneta' seed
1 x 50-cm/20-inch-diameter container
Multipurpose or soil-based compost
General organic vegetable fertilizer

GROW ME

SOW IN EARLY SPRING

- Choose a sunny, sheltered spot for the container. It is a good idea to divide the surface of the compost/fertilizer mix into three sections, one for each vegetable variety.
- Sow three broad bean seeds in a triangular shape, with one seed at each point, about 20 cm/8 inches apart and at a depth of about 5 cm/2 inches. Thinly scatter the carrot seed ('Caracas' is a short-rooted, Chantenay type) and cover with a 1-cm/½-inch layer of sieved soil or of vermiculite.
- Beetroot may be sown a little deeper, at 2 cm/¾ inches, and as the seeds are bigger you can make individual sowing holes with a pencil or the tip of a dibber and sow two seeds in each one. Try to space them about 7–10 cm/ 3–4 inches apart, but, as with all container vegetables, it is fine if they are a bit more snug.
- Once the carrot seedlings are large enough to handle, thin them to ensure that they have sufficient room to grow, to 7–10 cm/ 3–4 inches apart. The earlier you can do this, the better, because the dreaded carrot fly is attracted by the scent of bruised leaves, which can be caused by thinning. However, there is a school of thought that container-grown carrots do not suffer so much because they are off the ground (carrot fly can only strike up to 60 cm/2 ft above ground level). Remove the weakest beetroot seedling from each sowing position when they reach about 5 cm/2 inches tall.

- In cool areas, protect the bean and carrots seedings from frost until after mid-spring. Water the container well and apply a balanced liquid fertilizer every two weeks (this carrot variety can stand a little more watering and feeding than other varieties, without forking).
- 'The Sutton' is a dwarf broad bean, so will not need staking. When the first beans appear, pinch out the growing tips to encourage other pods to set, to keep the beans tender and to deter blackfly.

TIME TO HARVEST

From midsummer, when bean pods are well filled and the beans are still soft, the carrots are sweet and crunchy and the beetroot are a little bigger than golf-ball-size and tender.

ROOM IN THE POT

Sow more beetroot to replace harvested carrots and beetroot, either for smaller beetroot in early autumn or for delicious, succulent leaves to use in salads.

EACH RECIPE SERVES TWO

BEETROOT HUMMUS

INGREDIENTS
250 g/9 oz cooked beetroot
1 × 440-g/15-oz tin cooked
  chickpeas
1 garlic clove, crushed
2 heaped tsp tahini
2 tbsp lemon juice
2 tsp ground cumin
Salt and pepper, to taste
100 ml/3½ fl oz olive oil

METHOD
- Place all the ingredients into a mixer and blitz until blended and smooth. Spoon into a bowl and level, to remove any air pockets.
- Serve immediately, with warm pitta bread, or cover with a film of olive oil to preserve it and store in the refrigerator.

CARROT HUMMUS

INGREDIENTS
200 g/7 oz carrots
Drizzle of olive oil
Salt and pepper, to taste
1 × 440-g/15-oz tin
  cooked chickpeas
1 garlic clove, crushed
2 heaped tsp tahini
2 tbsp lemon juice
2 tsp ground cumin

METHOD
- Preheat the oven to 200°C/400°F/gas mark 6.
- Place the carrots on a baking sheet, drizzle with olive oil and season. Roast in the oven until soft – about 30 minutes.
- When the carrots have cooked, place them and the remainder of the ingredients into a mixer and blitz until blended and smooth. Spoon into a bowl and level, to remove any air pockets.
- Serve immediately, with warm pitta bread, or cover with a film of olive oil to preserve it and store in the refrigerator.

BROAD BEAN HUMMUS

INGREDIENTS
400 g/14 oz broad beans,
  podded
2 handfuls of basil,
  chopped
1 garlic clove, crushed
1 heaped tsp tahini
1 tbsp lemon juice
Salt and pepper, to taste
Glug of olive oil

METHOD
- Quickly blanche the broad beans in a pan of salted, boiling water until tender. Drain and immediately plunge into a bowl of iced cold water.
- Remove the broad beans from their skins.
- Place all the ingredients (apart from the olive oil) into a mixer and blitz until blended.
- Add a glug of olive oil to help combine the ingredients. Spoon into a bowl and level, to remove any air pockets.
- Serve immediately, with warm pitta bread, or cover with a film of olive oil to preserve it and store in the refrigerator.

BABA GANOUSH

Smoky, smooth and sumptuous, baba ganoush is a marvellous dip that transforms aubergine from a spongy vegetable into a creamy, heavenly treat. The plants are pretty too: soft purple flowers appear in early summer, followed by either dark, sultry, almost black or striped violet-purple vegetables, depending on the variety. I have used 'Amethyst' in my pot, which has small, violet fruits; another good dwarf variety is 'Ophelia'. 'Cha Cha' chives add a bit of fun, with their swirly-topped leaves.

Aubergine flowers attract pollinating insects.

1 x packet of aubergine 'Amethyst' F1 seed
2 x chive 'Cha Cha'
2 x apple mint (*Mentha* x *gracilis*)
1 x 45-cm/18-inch-diameter container
Multipurpose or soil-based compost
General organic vegetable fertilizer

POT RECIPE

GROW ME

SOW IN LATE WINTER; PLANT IN SPRING

- Prepare a seed tray with compost. Thinly sow a handful of aubergine seed and cover with a thin layer of compost (about 5 mm/¼ inch). Place on a windowsill or in a heated greenhouse or conservatory – the seed needs a temperature of 15–20°C (59–68°F) to germinate.

- When the seedlings are large enough to handle, pot on into 9-cm/3½-inch pots. When flowers start to appear in spring, they are ready to be transplanted to their final positions in a sunny, sheltered spot.

- Plant two aubergines, about 35 cm/14 inches apart, in the middle of the prepared container. Plant a chive next to each aubergine. Pot two mints, individually in 13-cm/5-inch pots to restrict their vigorous growth, and sink one pot on each side of the container.

- As the aubergine is a dwarf variety, there is no need to stake the plants. It is also a good idea to limit the crop to three to four fruits from each plant for the best results, so pick off the surplus flowers. Do not let the compost dry out and feed every week, once flowers appear, with a proprietary feed. Mist the aubergines every day to help the fruits set.

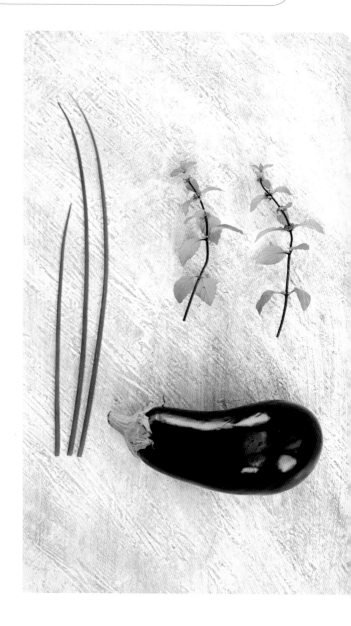

EAT ME

BABA GANOUSH

SERVES FOUR

INGREDIENTS

4 small or 3 medium-sized
  aubergines
2 tbsp tahini
2 garlic cloves, crushed
Juice of 1 lemon
1 handful of mint, chopped
1 tbsp chives, chopped
Salt and pepper, to taste
2 tbsp olive oil

METHOD

- Char the aubergines over a gas
  burner, turning them regularly
  to ensure that they cook evenly
  and all the flesh is soft and
  collapsing. (If you do not have
  a gas hob, poke the aubergines
  all over with a sharp knife and
  bake on a foil-lined baking
  sheet in a preheated oven at
  180°C/350°F/gas mark 4 for
  15 minutes. Place a damp tea
  towel over the hot aubergines
  to steam off the skins.)
- Set the aubergines aside to cool.
- Scoop out the aubergine flesh
  and squeeze it to release excess
  moisture. Discard the skins.
- Put the rest of the ingredients,
  apart from the oil, into a bowl
  and mix. Season to taste.
- Roughly mash the aubergine
  flesh and add to the rest of the
  ingredients and mix well.
- Pour over the oil and serve with
  pitta bread, crudités or thinly
  sliced, toasted sourdough.

TIME TO HARVEST

Thankfully, 'Amethyst' aubergine
will not produce thorns (unless
stressed), making the late-summer
harvest less prickly that it would
be from one of its cousins. Snip the
heads off the chives and use the
leaves in the same way as traditional
varieties. Regularly pick the mint too,
to keep it neat and compact.

HONEY & THYME BLACKBERRIES WITH THYME SHORTBREADS

Pot-grown blackberries are just the ticket if you live in the city and it is hard to get out and find those fruit-laden hedgerows that are the stuff of childhood memories. Low-growing thymes give the display extra interest and are another treat for pollinating insects, but from a culinary perspective they elevate this sweet, juicy fruit from a child's treat to a grown-up indulgence. This is a quick and easy container to plant.

Blackberry and thyme flowers are an early-summer treat for bees and other pollinating insects.

POT RECIPE

1 x blackberry 'Navaho Bigandearly'
2 x *Thymus pulegioides* 'Archer's Gold'
2 x *Thymus vulgaris* 'Compactus'
1 x 50-cm/20-inch-diameter container
Multipurpose or soil-based compost
General organic vegetable fertilizer
Horticultural grit
5 x 125-cm/4-ft bamboo canes and twine

GROW ME   PLANT IN LATE WINTER (bare-root) OR EARLY SPRING (container-grown)

- This blackberry pot is a really useful addition to your edible container garden, because it can cope in a bit of shade, just as it can in full sun. However, expect fruits later in the season if it does not see much sun.
- As well as the fertilizer, mix several handfuls of horticultural grit into the compost to provide a good, free-draining medium that both the blackberry and the thymes will appreciate.
- Plant the blackberry in the centre of the pot to give the roots plenty of room to get established. Support the blackberry stems with a wigwam of bamboo canes. Make

a figure-of-eight between the stem and the bamboo cane to protect the stems from being damaged. Cut off the bottom of a 500-ml/18-fl oz plastic water bottle and push the neck of the bottle into the soil behind the blackberry. Water through this bottle to help direct the water to the blackberry's roots.

- Repot the thymes into 13-cm/5-inch pots in a 50:50 mix of compost and horticultural grit – thymes do not like having wet feet and this will help to reduce their exposure to the wetter soil that the blackberry needs. Plunge their pots into the container, alternating varieties of thyme, 15 cm/6 inches apart in front of the blackberry.

- Water and feed the blackberry regularly. Do not water the pots containing the thymes directly: they should get all the moisture they need from the compost in the main container.

- Once blackberries have been harvested, cut back the fruited canes to soil level. Tie in new stems to the supports.

PERENNIAL POT

This container of perennials will not leave any gaps once its crops have been harvested. However, you will need to repot the blackberry plant after a few years.

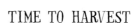

TIME TO HARVEST

Blackberry 'Navaho Bigandearly' is a winner because, as its name suggests, it produces large, juicy fruits that are ready from mid- to late summer. Thyme may be picked all year round.

EAT ME

HONEY & THYME BLACKBERRIES WITH THYME SHORTBREADS

SERVES FOUR

INGREDIENTS

110 g/4 oz unsalted butter
50 g/1¾ oz raw cane sugar
100 g/3½ oz plain flour
50 g/1¾ oz cornflour
Pinch of salt
Seeds of half a vanilla pod
1½ tbsp thyme leaves,
    finely chopped
400 g/14 oz blackberries,
    washed
2 tbsp honey

METHOD

- First, make the twelve shortbread biscuits. Cream the butter and sugar together until completely amalgamated. Slowly add the two flours, salt, vanilla and ½ tbsp thyme leaves. Mix well into a biscuit dough.
- On a floured surface, roll the dough out to a 5-mm/¼-inch thickness. Cut out biscuit shapes with a cookie cutter, 5 cm/2 inches in diameter. Place on a baking sheet lined with non-stick baking paper. Chill the biscuits in the refrigerator for 30 minutes.
- In a heavy-based saucepan cook the blackberries with the honey and 1 tbsp thyme leaves until the fruit is soft and beginning to run in colour. Set the pan aside, off the heat.
- Preheat the oven to 180°C/350°F/gas mark 4.
- Take the shortbread biscuits from the refrigerator and bake for 20 minutes, until completely cooked but still golden and not browned. Serve with the cooked blackberries.

Frittata & microgreens salad

Beetroot soup

Gazpacho

Toby's garden salad

SOUPS & SALADS

Kale & celery soup

FRITTATA & MICROGREENS SALAD

This is a great idea if you do not have a lot of space for growing vegetables, or the patience to wait for seedlings to develop over the course of a typical growing season. Microgreens seed may be sown on damp kitchen paper and will produce a delicious crop in a matter of days! It is worth growing a few varieties together, to give you a colourful display and plenty of interesting and intense flavours to add a zing to dishes. Use them wherever and whenever you can, to add a punch of flavour to sandwiches, to scatter on a salad or over tarts and flans or to garnish meat and fish. Keep the container shallow to reduce the amount of compost you need – if you are not fussy about the display, you can even use lengths of guttering – but remember to put the plastic end caps on to prevent the compost from spilling out.

POT RECIPE

1 x packet of daikon radish 'Longipinnatus' seed
1 x packet of mustard 'Red Giant' seed
1 x packet of purple Japanese beefsteak (*Perilla*) seed
1 x packet of coriander (*Coriandrum sativum*) seed
1 x 20-cm/8-inch-diameter and 10-cm/4-inch-deep
   container or growbag
Multipurpose or soil-based compost

GROW ME
SOW LATE SPRING TO AUTUMN

- Choose a sunny, sheltered spot for your shallow container or growbag. Gently water the compost prior to sowing seed so you do not risk moving the seed around with the force of the water: you want to achieve a nice, even distribution when the seed starts to germinate.
- Use the seed of the different varieties to create a pattern for your microgreens display – scatter each type of seed in lines, spots or waves – until the surface is completely covered. Cover with a fine layer of vermiculite.

ROOM IN THE POT

Successionally sow seed to replace the harvested microgreens and you will have a steady supply of fresh pickings from late spring well into autumn (and winter, if you move them on to a windowsill).

Start using the microgreens once they are about 5 cm/2 inches tall – anywhere from one to two weeks after sowing.

Simply use a pair of scissors to cut the young leaves – you will not believe the intense flavours of this crop!

EAT ME

FRITTATA & MICROGREENS SALAD

SERVES FOUR

INGREDIENTS
8 free-range eggs
Sea salt and pepper, to taste
200 ml/7 fl oz milk
Butter
1 handful of microgreens

METHOD
- Preheat the oven to 180°C/350°F/gas mark 4.
- Whisk the eggs, sea salt, pepper and milk together in a bowl. Butter a 1-litre/2-pint ovenproof or baking dish and pour the egg mixture into it.
- Bake for 15–20 minutes, until fully cooked and browned on the top.
- Top with the microgreens and serve.

TOBY'S GARDEN SALAD

Named after the rather brilliant Toby Connabeer, who is the horticultural guru at Suttons and was more than a help with this book. He eats vegetables and salads on the hoof, checking the crops he is growing and grazing all the while! It seemed appropriate to combine a few of his favourite varieties – and a few new leaves – for a seasonal treat that will keep on cropping until the autumn. Feel free to play fast and loose with your own combination of favourite leaves and herbs. The essential idea is to keep a container close to the kitchen door filled with a tempting array of fresh leaves that you can throw in a dish, add a dressing and serve … Nice and easy!

POT RECIPE

1 x packet of shiso 'Green' (*Perilla*) seed
1 x packet of purple Japanese beefsteak (*Perilla*) seed
1 x packet of Thai basil (*Ocimum* x *africanum* 'Siam Queen') seed
1 x packet of lettuce 'Red Salad Bowl' seed
1 x packet of lettuce 'Salad Bowl' seed
1 x packet of radicchio 'Palla Rossa' seed
1 x packet of sorrel 'Blood Veined' (*Rumex*) seed
1 x 40-cm/16-inch-diameter container
Multipurpose or soil-based compost
General organic vegetable fertilizer

GROW ME

SOW IN EARLY AND LATE SPRING

- In early spring, prepare two seed trays and one modular tray with compost. Thinly sow both types of perilla in one seed tray, covering it with a fine layer of compost. Sow the Thai basil seed in another, scattering it evenly across the compost surface, and covering it with vermiculite.
- Sow both varieties of lettuce in the modular tray, two in each cell (thin to the strongest seedling when they appear). Place the trays in the greenhouse or make room for them on a windowsill.
- In late spring, prepare a 9-cm/3½-inch pot and sow two or three radicchio seeds in it. Cover with a thin layer of compost and place in a greenhouse or on a windowsill. When the seedlings are

large enough to handle, thin to the strongest seedling.

- Place the container in a position in full sun, then fill with compost mixed with fertilizers. Transplant one radicchio plant to one side of the pot.
- Also in late spring, direct-sow a few sorrel seeds on the opposite side of the pot to the radicchio, about 1 cm/½ inch deep. When the seedlings are large enough, thin to leave the strongest seedling.
- When the remainder of the seedlings are large enough to handle and any risk of frosts has passed, plant them out in the container. Keep the perilla seedlings at the back, one green and one purple type, with one basil plant between them. Plant three plants of each variety of lettuce, in alternating colours, around the front of the pot.
- Do not let the container dry out and watch out for slugs and snails with this container: it is a veritable feast of tasty, tender leaves. Slug pellets are fine, but you cannot beat the night-time vigil, torch in hand, to be sure you keep the container pest-free. Feed every two weeks with a compound fertilizer – these plants want nitrogen, potash and phosphorus!

ROOM IN THE POT

Continue to sow the lettuces successively until early autumn to transplant into the container as and when needed. This will keep the display providing a crop well into autumn, with some leaves continuing over the winter, but give some protection to see the plants through the winter months.

TIME TO HARVEST

Pick leaves as you wish – as a cut-and-come-again crop from early summer or allow the lettuces to form heads in late summer. The radicchio will provide a new flavour in the salad at the end of the summer into autumn, when it is ready to harvest.

EAT ME

SERVES TWO AS A SIDE SALAD

INGREDIENTS
3 handfuls of shiso
    'Green' (*Perilla*) leaves,
    finely chopped
3 handfuls of purple
    Japanese beefsteak (*Perilla*)
    leaves, finely chopped
3 large handfuls of
    lettuce leaves
1 handful of sorrel leaves
2 sprigs of Thai basil
Radicchio (when available)
Glug of olive oil
Splash of balsamic vinegar
Salt and pepper, to taste

METHOD
• Wash and put the salad
  leaves in a bowl.
• Finely chop the Thai basil
  and add to the leaves.
• For this recipe you could
  use just a few young,
  outer radicchio leaves,
  but if you want to harvest
  the whole heart, let the
  radicchio mature. Then
  you can make it more of
  a meal and use it in one,
  generous salad.
• Dress with olive oil and
  balsamic vinegar and
  season to taste.

KALE & CELERY SOUP

This is the perfect autumnal soup, packed with nutrients
and goodness thanks to the gorgeously green ingredients.
While each vegetable has a distinct flavour, when they are
combined they produce a deliciously earthy flavour. It is a
great container for a patio display too, with its strong combination
of textures and tones. If you have enough growing space, you can
make the soup a more intense green by adding spinach leaves
(sow in mid-spring in a growbag and simply add freshly picked
leaves to the soup along with the celery and kale).

POT
RECIPE

1 x packet of kale 'Nero di Toscana' seed
3 x packet of celery 'Golden Self-blanching 3' seed
1 x packet of flat leaf parsley (*Petroselinum crispum*
'Plain Leaved 2') seed
1 x packet of pot marigold (*Calendula officinalis*
'Indian Prince') seed
1 x 40-cm/16-inch-diameter container
Multipurpose or soil-based compost
General organic vegetable fertilizer

GROW ME

SOW IN EARLY SPRING; PLANT IN LATE SPRING

- Sow the kale, celery, parsley and pot
marigold seed – three or four evenly
spaced seeds in each 9-cm/3½-inch pot.
Lightly cover the seed with compost
and keep in a greenhouse or on a sunny
windowsill. When the seedlings are large
enough to handle, pot on into individual
pots and return to a greenhouse or a
sunny windowsill.

- In late spring, place the container in a
sunny, sheltered position and prepare
with compost and the appropriate mix
of fertilizer. Transplant the seedlings:

three celery at the back of the pot, kale
and parsley in front of the celery, one on
either side of the pot and a pot marigold
at the very front of the pot in the centre.

- Water the container well after planting
and apply a balanced liquid fertilizer
every two weeks.

- The celery is a self-blanching variety,
so will not need to be earthed up. Pick
the parsley regularly to encourage fresh
growth and a neat habit. Deadhead the
pot marigold regularly to encourage new
flowers and extend the season.

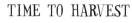

TIME TO HARVEST

The celery and kale will be ready to harvest from mid-autumn. The parsley and pot marigold flowers may be picked and used from early summer. If you grow spinach to add to this recipe, that may be picked until the autumn too.

EAT ME

KALE & CELERY SOUP

SERVES FOUR

INGREDIENTS
4 tbsp olive oil
1 onion, finely chopped
1 garlic clove, finely chopped
Pinch each of sea salt and pepper, to taste
4 celery sticks, finely chopped
500 g/18 oz kale leaves
200 g/7 oz spinach leaves, trimmed
2 handfuls of parsley, chopped
1.25 litres/2 pints 4 fl oz of
    vegetable stock
1 handful of pot marigold petals

METHOD
- In a heavy-bottomed soup pot, heat the olive oil and sauté the onion and garlic until soft. Add sea salt and pepper to encourage the onion to soften without burning.
- Add the celery pieces and mix well. Remove the stalks from the kale leaves, finely chop and add them to the pot. Mix well.
- Add the spinach leaves and parsley. Mix and add the stock.
- Simmer the soup for 20 minutes. Allow to cool slightly; blend to a fine purée and sieve.
- Garnish with a celery leaf and serve with crusty bread. Alternatively, scatter marigold petals onto the soup seconds before serving.

SOUPS & SALADS ● 71

BEETROOT SOUP

Leave some of the coriander plants to flower, to give bees and other pollinators a summer treat.

A colourful, quick-growing container that makes the most beautifully vibrant soup that is packed with nutrients. Beetroot is easy to grow and offers great value for money because you can eat the young tender leaves as well as the root. The bright red veins and stems look a treat against the frothy, lush green foliage of the 'Confetti' coriander, making it work as an ornamental display. The soup is simple and delicious – the beetroot will thicken on its own so there is no need to add potatoes, saving on peeling time!

POT RECIPE

1 x packet of beetroot 'Moneta' seed
1 x packet of *Coriandrum sativum* 'Confetti' seed
1 x *Thymus vulgaris* 'Compactus'
1 x 30-cm/12-inch-diameter container
Multipurpose or soil-based compost
General organic vegetable fertilizer
Horticultural grit

GROW ME

SOW AND PLANT IN MID-SPRING

- Fill a container in a sunny, sheltered spot with compost, water well and divide the container into three sections for sowing.
- Sow the beetroot seed at 5-cm/2-inch intervals, dotted in a random pattern over two-thirds of the compost surface. This is much tighter than traditional spacing in rows and will result in smaller beets, but they will be sweet and delicious when you harvest them. Also, sowing in this way will provide a lush coverage of red-veined beetroot leaves and make an attractive display.

- Sow six to eight coriander seeds in the remaining third section, leaving a space for the thyme at the front of the pot. Cover with a fine dusting of compost (about 5 mm/¼ inch deep).
- Add a few handfuls of horticultural grit to the planting hole of the thyme and plant it, firming well.
- Once they are large enough, thin the coriander seedlings to three strong seedlings, equally spaced. Keep the container well watered (daily during the height of summer) and feed weekly.

ROOM IN THE POT

Once beet harvesting begins, you could sow more coriander or try something different, such as the quick-growing spinach 'Lazio', in batches until late summer to use in soups or as young, tender salad leaves.

TIME TO HARVEST

Beetroots will be ready to harvest from midsummer. Coriander may be harvested as early as twenty-eight days after sowing, to obtain young, tender leaves, or left on the plant to mature.

EAT ME

SERVES FOUR

INGREDIENTS
400 g/14 oz beetroot,
   boiled until soft with
   their skins on
Knob of butter
100 g/3½ oz onion, chopped
2 sprigs of thyme
Salt and pepper, to taste
1 litre/35 fl oz of vegetable
   or chicken stock
1 handful of coriander
   leaves, roughly chopped

METHOD
• Remove the skins from the cooked beetroot and
  chop roughly.
• Add a knob of butter to a saucepan and sauté the
  beetroot and onions over a medium heat. Add the leaves
  from the thyme sprigs (run your fingers downwards
  along the length of the stems to remove the leaves
  easily). When the butter foams, season and cover with a
  lid for about ten minutes.
• Add the stock and bring to the boil.
• Blitz in a blender until smooth and check the
  seasoning again.
• At the last minute before serving, garnish with the
  chopped coriander leaves.

GAZPACHO

The combination of tomato, sweet pepper and cucumber flowers is irresistible to pollinating insects.

Growing tomatoes can be a bit hit and miss in cool climates. It is not unusual to have a glut of green, unripened fruits at the end of the growing season – which thankfully make a delicious chutney. However, choose an appropriate variety and you will be headed for success and a delicious, Mediterranean-style dish like this gazpacho will be within reach. This refreshing summer soup really benefits from home-grown tomatoes; plum types are best. 'Giulietta' is useful for cooler climates: its fruits set and ripen well even in cooler temperatures. Similarly, mini-cucumber 'Rocky' is happy in cooler conditions; also, it produces only female flowers, which means that you will not have to worry about pinching off male flowers to keep the fruits sweet. The sweet pepper and cucumber add texture and flavour to the soup, as well as providing contrasts of height and habit in the container display. Add some garlic to provide foliage texture, along with a delicious zing to the finished dish.

POT RECIPE

2 x garlic 'Sultop' cloves
1 x packet of sweet pepper 'Corno di Toro Rosso' seed
1 x packet of tomato 'Giulietta' F1 seed
1 x packet of cucumber 'Rocky' F1 seed
1 x 50-cm/20-inch-diameter container
Multipurpose or soil-based compost
General organic vegetable fertilizer

GROW ME   SOW IN LATE WINTER AND SPRING; PLANT IN EARLY SUMMER

- If you have space to start this pot off in late winter, then it is worth getting the garlic cloves in early. Position and prepare the container in a sunny, sheltered spot.
- Plant the cloves near the edge of the pot on one side, leaving about 10 cm/4 inches between each clove and ensuring their tips are just beneath the compost surface. Otherwise, wait until early spring.

- In early spring, sow a few sweet pepper seeds into 9-cm/3½-inch pots. Thin to the strongest seedling when they are large enough to handle. This crop needs warmth: leave in a heated greenhouse if possible at 21–4°C/70–75°F or on a warm windowsill.
- Four weeks later, sow the tomato seed in the same way.

- A month after that, sow two or three cucumber seeds individually in 9-cm/ 3½-inch pots.
- In early summer, once the risk of frost has passed, transplant one of each crop into the container already planted with garlic. Plant the tomato at the back of the container, with the sweet pepper and cucumber at the front, one on each side.
- Pinch out the tomato side shoots as they grow and stake the tomato and sweet pepper, to support the swelling fruits. Allow the cucumber to trail, pinching out the growing tips if needed to keep the stems within bounds. Water well and feed weekly with tomato fertilizer.

TIME TO HARVEST

Staggering the sowing dates helps the garlic and fruits to ripen together, ready for harvest from mid- to late summer. Spring-sown garlic may also be lifted as early as midsummer, although the bulbs will be a bit smaller than if left until the leaves have yellowed, indicating that the bulbs are fully mature. You can also continue to harvest the leftover fruits right into early to late autumn.

SERVES FOUR

INGREDIENTS
2 garlic cloves
1 tsp cumin seeds
Pinch each of salt and pepper
Glug of olive oil
Splash of white wine vinegar
1 shallot, finely sliced
1 handful of chervil leaves,
    finely chopped
250 ml/9 fl oz iced water
6 ripe tomatoes
1 sweet red pepper
1 small cucumber,
    peeled and diced
2 handfuls of white bread,
    roughly chopped

METHOD
- Prepare a dressing by grinding the garlic, cumin, salt and pepper in a pestle and mortar. Blend with the glug of olive oil and the white wine vinegar. Add the shallot, chervil and iced water. Taste and adjust the seasoning if necessary.
- Thinly slice the tomato and sweet pepper and cover with the dressing. Leave to marinade for ten minutes.
- Add the cucumber and bread and a little more water, if necessary.
- Before serving, add a couple of ice cubes to ensure that the soup is chilled.

Carrot pesto

Rainbow chard pesto

Garden pizza

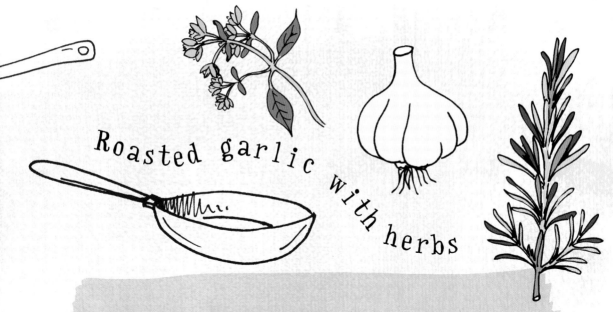

Roasted garlic with herbs

QUICK SUPPERS

Simple ratatouille

CARROT PESTO

Impress your friends and serve an orange-coloured pesto rather than the more traditional green type. Sweet and earthy, this makes a tasty change and is a great way to tempt little ones to eat carrots if they are not sold on them in their raw state. I have chosen a Chantenay-type carrot, which is short-rooted, so suits this size of container. Add a zing to the display, and indeed the finished dish, with eye-catching nasturtiums, which have an attractive trailing habit and two-tone, peppery-tasting flowers.

Nasturtium flowers are great for pollinating insects.

POT RECIPE

12 x garlic 'Sultop' cloves
1 x packet of carrot 'Caracas' seed
1 x packet of nasturtium 'Banana Split' seed
1 x 45-cm/18-inch-diameter container
Multipurpose or soil-based compost
General organic vegetable fertilizer

GROW ME

SOW AND PLANT IN EARLY SPRING

- Place the container in a sheltered, sunny spot.
- Plant the garlic cloves in double rows across the centre of the container. Firm the soil either side of the garlic and water gently. Make a drill for the carrots on each side of the garlic. Sow fairly thinly to avoid having to thin them out much when the seedlings emerge – the scent of bruised leaves attracts the dreaded carrot fly. Sow a few nasturtium seeds at the front of the container, about 2 cm/¾ inch deep.
- Remove the weakest nasturtium seedlings, when they are large enough to handle, leaving two to grow on.
- Water regularly to prevent the container from drying out. Feed every two weeks.

TIME TO HARVEST

Both the carrots and garlic will be ready to harvest in midsummer. Yellowing garlic leaves indicate that they have reached maturity; lift the carrots as needed for the pesto. Harvest the nasturtium leaves and flowers as they appear, to add colour to salads and then, when you have made the pesto, to add even more colour to the dish.

EAT ME

SERVES FOUR TO SIX

INGREDIENTS

8 carrots, peeled and finely chopped
3 garlic cloves, chopped
2 tbsp olive oil (and a drizzle to roast
    the vegetables)
Salt and pepper, to taste
75 g/2½ oz whole almonds
Juice of half a lemon
75 g/2½ oz Parmesan cheese, chopped into
    small pieces
Chives or microgreens, for garnish
1 handful of nasturtium
    flowers

METHOD

- Preheat the oven to 180°C/350°F/gas
  mark 4.
- Place the carrots and garlic in a roasting
  dish and lightly drizzle with olive oil.
  Season. Roast for 15 minutes or so until
  soft. Allow to cool.
- Transfer the mixture into a blender, add
  the almonds, lemon juice, Parmesan and
  the 2 tbsp olive oil and blitz into a paste.
  Spoon into a bowl and level, to remove
  any air pockets.
- Serve immediately or seal the pesto with
  a film of olive oil and cover with clingfilm
  before storing in the refrigerator.
- Just before serving, garnish the top of the
  pesto with chives or microgreens to add
  zing and use the colourful nasturtium
  flowers to decorate the serving dish.

RAINBOW CHARD PESTO

Perfect for introducing colour into your garden, rainbow chard tastes as good as it looks. It is a great cropper too, producing delicious leaves and stems that can be harvested all year, simply by cutting down the whole plant during warm, summer months. New leaves will shoot in three to four weeks. It is best to harvest just the outer leaves during winter months. Chard and garlic is a classic combination, and this recipe makes a nice change to basil pesto, tasting a bit more earthy. If you want an even easier dish than pesto, cook both vegetables in butter, season well and serve over pasta or simply on their own!

POT
RECIPE

12 x garlic 'Sultop'
    cloves
1 x packet of chard
    'Bright Lights' seed
1 x 50-cm/ 20-inch-
    diameter container
Multipurpose or soil-
    based compost
General organic
    vegetable fertilizer

- Place and prepare the container in a sunny, sheltered spot.
- It is best to plant the garlic first in late winter, in a double row across the middle of the container. Make each hole about 2.5 cm/1 inch deep and cover the cloves so that their points sit just beneath the surface of the compost. Gently firm the soil on either side of the garlic rows, in preparation for sowing the rainbow chard, and water them in well.
- In mid-spring, dot a series of holes, about 1 cm/½ inch deep, in rows across the front and back of the container. Sow two or three chard seeds in each hole and cover with compost.
- Once the chard germinates, thin each position to one seedling, choosing the strongest contender. Water regularly and feed every week.

TIME TO HARVEST

By midsummer the garlic and chard may be harvested to make the pesto.

ROOM IN THE POT

Treat the remaining chard as a cut-and-come-again crop that will continue to provide salad leaves after the garlic has been harvested for this recipe.

EAT ME

RAINBOW CHARD PESTO

SERVES FOUR

INGREDIENTS
4 large handfuls of rainbow chard
    leaves, rough stalks trimmed
2 garlic cloves, chopped
1 handful of walnuts
75 g/2½ oz pecorino cheese, chopped
    into small pieces
100 ml/3½ fl oz olive oil
Salt and pepper, to taste

METHOD
- Sauté the rainbow chard leaves and garlic in a
  heavy-based pan. Drain and allow to cool.
- Transfer the vegetables into a blender and add
  the walnuts and pecorino, blitzing the mixture
  to a rough paste.
- Mix in the olive oil and blend further. Spoon
  the pesto into a bowl and level, to remove any
  air pockets.
- Season to taste and serve immediately or seal
  the pesto with a film of olive oil and cover with
  clingfilm before storing it in the refrigerator.

GARDEN PIZZA

Tomato and herb flowers will tempt bees and other pollinating insects to visit your garden.

You cannot beat the flavour of a home-made pizza base and what could be more satisfying than growing the ingredients for the topping. The secret to success is keeping the topping simple and not too moist – fresh herbs and young leaves like rocket, sorrel or spinach work really well with the traditional staple of tomato and cheese. For an extra kick, scatter a handful of thinly sliced fresh chilli on the top. Why not grow a couple of these containers with a different-coloured tomato as the centrepiece in each – try yellow 'Sungold' F1 or black 'Indigo Rose' – and change the accompanying herbs and leaves.

POT RECIPE

1 x packet of tomato 'Baby Sweet' seed
1 x marjoram (*Origanum majorana*)
1 x oregano/pot marjoram (*Origanum vulgare*)
1 x basil (*Ocimum* 'African Blue')
1 x 45-cm/18-inch-diameter container
Multipurpose or soil-based compost
Horticultural grit
General organic vegetable fertilizer

GROW ME

SOW IN EARLY SPRING; PLANT IN LATE SPRING

- In early spring, sow 2–3 tomato seeds in a 9-cm/3½-inch pot. When they have two true leaves, thin to the strongest seedling to grow on. Tomatoes benefit from warmth, so leave the pot in a heated greenhouse if possible (at 21–4°C/ 70–75°F) or on a sunny windowsill.
- In late spring after the risk of frosts has passed or in early summer, prepare the container in a sunny, sheltered spot. Plant one tomato at the back of the container and plant the three herbs in the remaining space.

- Pinch out the side shoots of the tomato as it grows, to encourage it to form a tall plant, and tie in to canes for support once the fruits start to appear.
- It is important to water the tomato consistently to avoid blossom end rot spoiling the fruits. Cut off the end of a plastic water bottle and plunge the neck of it into the soil by the tomato. Water into this to reach the tomato roots rather than soaking the top of the container and waterlogging the herbs. Feed the tomato weekly with dilute tomato fertilizer.

- Pick the herbs regularly to keep them producing young, fresh leaves.
- At the end of the growing season, remove the tomato plant. The basil, oregano and marjoram will overwinter with a little care and protection: if temperatures drop or there is a risk of frost, protect them with horticultural fleece or move them into a greenhouse or shed. The following season, sow more tomatoes to plant into the container again.

TIME TO HARVEST

The herbs will be ready to harvest before the tomatoes ripen, so make use of them in other dishes. Herbs really benefit from regularly picking because it encourages new growth and keeps the plants attractively neat, as opposed to leggy and straggling. By midsummer, if the sun has been shining, the tomatoes should be ready to harvest.

MAKES TWO 25-CM/10-INCH PIZZAS

INGREDIENTS

PIZZA BASE
500 g/18 oz strong white flour
7 g/¼ oz dried yeast
2 tbsp olive oil
1 tsp salt
325 ml/11½ fl oz warm water

TOMATO SAUCE
Glug of olive oil
1 garlic clove, finely grated
500 g/18 oz tomatoes, diced
¼ tsp unrefined granulated sugar
Salt and pepper, to taste

TOPPING
125 g/4½ oz mozzarella cheese
1 handful of marjoram leaves
1 handful of oregano leaves
1 handful of basil leaves
Black pepper, to taste

METHOD

- Mix all the ingredients for the pizza base (apart from the water) into a bowl. Then slowly add the water and mix to form a dough. Sprinkle some flour on the work surface and pour out the dough. Knead it for about ten minutes until the dough becomes quite elastic.
- Transfer it into a bowl, cover with a damp cloth (or tea towel) and leave for one and a half hours or until it rises to twice its size.
- Knock back the dough and knead for a further ten minutes. Leave in the bowl to rise again for an hour or so.
- Preheat the oven to its highest setting or a bread-making setting (usually 200–220°C/400–25°F/gas mark 7). Divide the dough mixture into two and roll each piece out on a floured surface to about 25 cm/10 inches in diameter.
- To make the sauce, heat the olive oil in a saucepan and sauté the garlic without letting it burn. Add the tomatoes, sugar and seasoning. Bring to the boil and let it simmer over a low heat for about 45 minutes, until it is reduced. Allow to cool and blitz in a blender to make it smooth.
- Spread 4 tbsp of tomato sauce over each pizza (freeze any leftover sauce or use it with pasta for another simple supper).
- Add chunks of mozzarella and cook the pizzas until the bases are crisp and golden and the cheese is starting to melt.
- Remove the cooked pizzas from the oven, scatter the freshly picked herb leaves over them, season with black pepper and serve.

ROASTED GARLIC WITH HERBS

Herb flowers entice pollinating insects of all types to pay a visit.

Nothing quite beats the look, taste and smell of roasted garlic straight from the oven – singed on the edges with an oozing, soft, gooey filling of subtle garlicky flavour. It is a great starter to share with friends – just cut a couple of bulbs in half and encourage them to pop the spreadable cloves on to a thin layer of sourdough toast. Simple, quick and delicious! The ingredients are easy to grow and you can keep this container of herbs going year after year, planting garlic cloves each season. You will have to repot the herbs after a few years, but otherwise this display will pretty much take care of itself.

POT RECIPE

6 x garlic 'Sultop' cloves
1 x *Rosmarinus officinalis*
1 x *Thymus* 'Silver Posie'
1 x oregano/pot marjoram (*Origanum vulgare*)
1 x 40-cm/16-inch-diameter container
Multipurpose or soil-based compost
General organic vegetable fertilizer
Horticultural grit

GROW ME

PLANT IN LATE WINTER TO EARLY SPRING

- If you have space to start this pot off in late winter, then it is worth getting the garlic cloves in nice and early. Position the container in a sunny, sheltered spot.
- Plant the cloves in a zigzag line across the middle of the pot to maximize the growing space (about 10 cm/4 inches) between each clove. After all, garlic is the hero of this recipe and the bigger the bulbs you can harvest, the better. Make sure to insert the cloves so that the tips are just beneath the compost surface. It is fine to wait until spring, when you will

have a good choice of small herb plants in your local garden centre or nursery, as well as having the satisfaction of planting the container in one go.

- When planting the herbs, add a few handfuls of horticultural grit at the bottom of each planting hole to aid drainage. Give the rosemary more room than the thyme and oregano, because it will be the largest plant in the display. Positioning it at the back is a good idea: it will act as a foil for the foliage of the other plants. The thyme and oregano can

TIME TO HARVEST

Do not wait until the garlic is ready before using the herbs – they really benefit from regular picking and just a few sprigs will improve your home-cooked dishes. Chefs recommend using garlic when it is small and 'wet', which is as early as late spring for this container. At this stage they are young and the texture is creamy – quite different from dried garlic – and their internal skins have not formed either, so it really lends itself to roasting. If you are serving this recipe for only small numbers, when a couple of garlic bulbs would be sufficient, it is worth giving it a try and lifting a few bulbs early. But if you need to feed a few more, it might be better to wait until the bulbs reach maturity towards the end of midsummer (keep an eye on their leaves, which will start to yellow and droop when ready to harvest). Perhaps the best idea is to try both options and, if you love the younger bulbs, next year try growing them in a couple of containers so you have plenty!

jostle for position at the front of the container.

- Water regularly so the pot does not dry out: drying out will affect the garlic more than the herbs, but do not let the herbs sit in waterlogged compost. Keep picking the herbs to encourage fresh, young leaves and to keep the plants healthy.

ROOM IN THE POT

Gaps are not a problem with this container because the herbs will happily fill any space once the garlic bulbs have been harvested.

EAT ME

ROASTED GARLIC WITH HERBS

SERVES FOUR

INGREDIENTS
1 garlic bulb
Glug of olive oil
2–3 sprigs each of oregano, rosemary and thyme
Sourdough (or your favourite) bread, thinly sliced

METHOD
- Preheat the oven to 180°C/350°F/gas mark 4.
- Cut the garlic bulb across the top to reveal the tips of the cloves. Put the garlic on a sheet of foil. Pour over the olive oil and add the herb sprigs. Fold the foil together over the garlic to make a sealed parcel.
- Bake in the oven for 45 minutes.
- Toast the sourdough slices and serve with the roasted garlic – invite your friends to spread a clove on each slice.

SIMPLE RATATOUILLE

A classic flavour combination, this also works really well as a container display because tomatoes, peppers and courgettes all need plenty of sun, food and water to produce a bountiful crop. There are lots of different versions of this dish: some are steeped in an unctuous tomato sauce, others lightly coated in oil and the juices of slow-roasted tomatoes, courgettes and sweet peppers. Feel free to change and tweak the core ingredients with your preferred vegetable varieties – perhaps a cherry rather than plum tomato or a traditional green or globe-shaped courgette instead of the yellow one used here.

An irresistible combination of courgette, tomato and pepper flowers is the perfect summer snack for bees and other pollinating insects.

POT RECIPE

1 x packet of tomato 'Giulietta' F1 seed
1 x packet of courgette 'Gold Star' F1 seed
1 x packet of aubergine 'Ophelia' F1 seed
1 x packet of sweet pepper 'Gypsy' F1 seed
1 x 50 x 100-cm/20 x 40-inch trough
Multipurpose or soil-based compost
General organic vegetable fertilizer

GROW ME   SOW IN MID-SPRING; PLANT IN LATE SPRING OR EARLY SUMMER

- Prepare one modular tray and sow seed of the tomato, courgette, aubergine and sweet pepper, one variety to one row of cells and two seeds per cell. Leave in a heated greenhouse or on a sunny windowsill at a temperature of 18–21°C/64–70°F to germinate.
- Once the seedlings in the modular tray are large enough to handle, prick out into 9-cm/3½-inch pots to grow on.
- In late spring, position the prepared trough in full sun in a sheltered spot. Transplant the strongest seedling of each variety. Position one tomato at the back

and insert a 1.75-m/6-ft cane next to it, ready to tie the plant in as it grows. Plant one courgette at the front of the pot; plant one sweet pepper and one aubergine between the tomato and the courgette.
- Pinch out any side shoots that appear between the tomato's stem and its fruit trusses; when the plant has produced five or six trusses, remove the growing tip. Support the stems once the aubergine, pepper and tomato flowers have set. Water regularly and use a proprietary feed once the first flowers have set.

This container will be ready to harvest from late summer, or slightly earlier given a hot summer with plenty of sunshine to let the tomatoes and aubergines ripen. Courgettes and sweet peppers may be harvested from early and midsummer and used for other dishes until it is time to add them to this recipe.

EAT ME

SIMPLE RATATOUILLE

SERVES FOUR

INGREDIENTS
200 ml/7 fl oz olive oil
2 onions, thinly sliced
4 garlic cloves, sliced
6 courgettes, thinly sliced
4 small or 2 large ripe sweet peppers, deseeded and thinly sliced
2 aubergines, thinly sliced and quartered
8 tomatoes, skinned, deseeded and quartered
2 bay leaves
2 sprigs of thyme
Salt and pepper, to taste

METHOD
• Preheat the oven to 180°C/350°F/ gas mark 4.
• Heat the oil in a large frying pan and sauté the onions until slightly brown. Add the garlic and cook for a few minutes until golden, but do not let the garlic burn.
• Add the courgettes, sweet peppers, aubergines and tomatoes. Add the herbs, season and bring to a simmer. Cover and cook for an hour.
• Eat warm or chilled (do not forget to remove the bay leaves and sprigs of thyme first!).

Salsa Verde

Chilli jam

Radish & shallot pickle

Bouquet garni

TASTY ACCOMPANIMENTS

Red cabbage & redcurrant pickle

SALSA VERDE

This beautiful, lush green container display combines the herbs
that form the basis of the classic green sauce salsa verde – a
delicious accompaniment to roasted or grilled meat or fish.
Inspired by the Italian version, which uses just parsley, this
recipe adds mint and basil to give a real depth of flavour.
Easy to grow and care for, this container is essential to the
cook-gardener's patio display.

**POT
RECIPE**

1 x spearmint (*Mentha spicata*)
2 x basil (*Ocimum* 'African Blue')
2 x flat leaf parsley (*Petroselinum crispum* 'Plain Leaved 2')
1 x 30-cm/12-inch-diameter container
Multipurpose or soil-based compost
General organic vegetable fertilizer

GROW ME   PLANT IN LATE SPRING OR EARLY SUMMER

- Although a sunny site is recommended for
  basil, this plant combination will cope in a
  part-shaded spot too, which makes this a
  useful container display.
- In late spring when the risk of frost has
  passed, or in early summer, pot on the
  mint into a 13-cm/5-inch pot and plunge
  the pot into the prepared container at the
  back. It is a bit of a thug, so it is a good
  idea to restrict its roots and give the
  other herbs in the container a chance
  to thrive too.
- At the same time, plant the two basil
  plants in the container, positioning them
  around the edge, so that each plant sits
  at two points of a triangle, with the mint
  at the third point. Then plant the two
  parsley plants in the gaps.

- Pinch out the tips of the herbs, to
  encourage bushy plants, and pick leaves
  regularly to encourage fresh, young
  growth. Do not overwater – basil in
  particular does not like sitting in soggy
  compost – but do not let the soil dry out.
  Feed with a high-nitrogen liquid fertilizer
  every two weeks.
- The basil, parsley and mint will
  overwinter with a little care and
  protection: if temperatures drop or there
  is a risk of frost, protect them with
  horticultural fleece or move them into a
  greenhouse or shed until the following
  spring or the risk of frost has passed.

TIME TO HARVEST

These herbs will be ready to start picking in quantity from midsummer; if you pick them regularly, they should continue to provide fresh leaves until the early autumn.

EAT ME

SALSA VERDE

SERVES SIX

INGREDIENTS
1 garlic clove
1 small handful of capers
1 small handful of pickled cornichons
6 anchovy fillets
I hard-boiled egg
2 large handfuls of flat leaf parsley
2 handfuls of fresh basil
1 handful of fresh mint
30 g/1 oz fresh breadcrumbs
1 tbsp Dijon mustard
1½ tbsp red wine vinegar
150 ml/5 fl oz extra-virgin olive oil
Salt and pepper, to taste

METHOD
- Finely chop the garlic, capers, cornichons, anchovies, boiled egg and herbs and put them in a bowl.
- Add the breadcrumbs, the mustard and the red wine vinegar and slowly stir in the olive oil.
- Season to taste and add a touch more red wine vinegar if needed.

RADISH & SHALLOT PICKLE

A great little pot that will not take up too much space and will provide you with the ingredients by midsummer to make a tangy, crunchy pickle as an addition to cold meats, cheeses and sandwiches. This recipe uses a mixture of red, pink and white radish, but purists can use traditional red-skinned types.

POT RECIPE

6 x shallot 'Pesandor' sets
1 x packet of radish 'French Breakfast 3' seed
1 x 30-cm/12-inch-diameter container
Multipurpose or soil-based compost
General organic vegetable fertilizer

GROW ME   PLANT IN EARLY SPRING; SOW IN LATE SPRING AND EARLY SUMMER

- Fill the container with compost and fertilizer in a sheltered, sunny spot.
- Use your finger (or dibber if you have one) to make a hole for each shallot set, in a zigzag pattern across the centre of the container. Make the holes just deep enough to allow the growing tips to peep just above the soil. Feel free to plant them a little more closely together than convention suggests: a 15-cm/ 6-inch space between them will give you slightly smaller bulbs.
- Direct-sow the radish seed in the container in early summer, sprinkling it all over the surface of the compost around the shallots – you should aim for a good, even coverage.
- Water the container well after sowing and as the plants grow.

TIME TO HARVEST

The shallots set the harvest date for this container. Wait until their leaves turn yellow and lift a week or so after. As both radish and shallots will be harvested and used for the pickle, do not worry too much about drying the shallots on the compost surface to let their skins harden – that is only necessary to help them to keep longer in storage.

EAT ME

RADISH & SHALLOT PICKLE

MAKES TWO 200-ML/7-FL OZ JARS

INGREDIENTS
150 ml/5 fl oz cider vinegar
150 ml/5 fl oz water
2 tsp salt
3 tbsp honey
20 radishes, thinly sliced
1 shallot, thinly sliced
1 tsp black peppercorns
1 tsp fennel seed

METHOD
- Sterilize the two preserving jars by heating them in the oven (lids separate) for ten minutes at 140°C/275°F/ gas mark 1.
- Add the cider vinegar, water, salt and honey to a saucepan and heat gently until the honey dissolves.
- Fill the jars with the radish, shallot, peppercorns and fennel seeds and pour the hot liquid into them.
- Seal with the lids, covering each lid with a disc of waxed paper and allow to cool.
- Leave for a day before eating; this pickle may be stored in the refrigerator for up to a month.

BOUQUET GARNI

No self-respecting chef would refuse the offer of a home-grown bouquet garni to add flavour to sauces and stews. It is a classic mixture in the kitchen and works brilliantly in the garden with a combination of perennial and annual herbs. Being leafy and herby, it looks great near the kitchen door ready to be picked. Feel free to use the herbs in other recipes too: these plants do benefit from regular harvesting throughout the season.

POT RECIPE

1 x 1-litre/13-cm pot of *Hyssopus officinalis*
1 x 1-litre/13-cm pot of bay (*Laurus nobilis*)
1 x 1-litre/13-cm pot of parsley (*Petroselinum crispum* 'Plain Leaved 2')
1 x 1-litre/13-cm pot of *Thymus vulgaris*
1 x 50-cm/20-inch-diameter container
Multipurpose or soil-based compost
Horticultural grit
General organic vegetable fertilizer

GROW ME

PLANT IN SPRING

- These herbs have the best flavour if grown in full sun, but give them a sheltered position. Prepare the container. Plant the hyssop at the back and the bay and parsley opposite each other across the middle, so these three herbs form the points of a triangle.
- Make a planting hole for the thyme at the front of the pot and add a couple of handfuls of horticultural grit to the bottom of the hole for extra drainage. Water in all the herbs well.
- Pick the herbs regularly to encourage plenty of new growth and to maintain a neat habit.

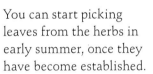

TIME TO HARVEST

You can start picking leaves from the herbs in early summer, once they have become established.

EAT ME

BOUQUET GARNI

SERVES FOUR

INGREDIENTS
1 bay leaf
2 sprigs of thyme
2 sprigs of parsley
1 sprig of hyssop

METHOD
• Wash the herbs.
• Simply tie the sprigs together with clean string and they are ready for use.
• This makes a bouquet garni to flavour a dish for four, but you can make a bigger bouquet to flavour larger quantities: for example simply double up the herbs for eight servings and triple it for twelve.

CHILLI JAM

A stylish yet simple container display, this packs a punch when it comes to the finished jam. It is the perfect, fiery accompaniment to all sorts of dishes – cheeses, cold meats and fishcakes providing a kick of flavour and a splash of colour. Chilli peppers are a popular vegetable to grow and, as long as they have lots of sunshine, will reward you with a plentiful and fiery crop.

POT RECIPE

1 x packet of chilli pepper 'Vampire' F1 seed
1 x packet of chilli pepper 'Krakatoa' F1 seed
1 x packet of chilli pepper 'Barak' seed
1 x packet of tomato 'Sweet Baby' seed
1 x oregano/pot marjoram *Origanum vulgare*
1 x 50-cm/20-inch-diameter container
Multipurpose or soil-based compost
General organic vegetable fertilizer

GROW ME

SOW IN EARLY SPRING; PLANT IN LATE SPRING

- Prepare one modular tray in early spring and sow all three varieties of chilli pepper, one variety to one row of cells and two seeds per cell. Sow the tomato seed, two seeds each into a couple of 9-cm/3½-inch pots. Leave the tray and pots in a heated greenhouse or on a sunny windowsill (these crops need 18–21°C/64–70°F to germinate).
- Once the chilli seedlings are large enough to handle, prick the strongest of each variety out into 9-cm/3½-inch pots.
- In late spring, once all risk of frosts has passed, prepare the container in a sunny, sheltered spot and plant one tomato in the centre. Put a 1.75-m/6-ft cane next to it, ready to tie into as the tomato grows. Plant three plants, one of each variety, of chilli in front of the tomato. Make a planting hole at the front of the pot; add a few handfuls of horticultural grit at the bottom to aid drainage and plant the oregano.
- Keep an eye on the growing tomato plant and pinch out any side shoots that appear between the main stem and the fruit trusses. Once the plant has produced five or six trusses, remove the growing tip. Support the chilli plants with canes as their fruits appear.
- Water the container regularly – not on the oregano – and use a tomato fertilizer (high in potassium) once all the plants' flowers set. Keep picking the oregano to encourage fresh, young leaves and to keep the plant compact and healthy.

TIME TO HARVEST

You can pick ingredients for this recipe from late summer, once all the crops have ripened.

EAT ME

CHILLI JAM

MAKES THREE
200-ML/7-FL OZ JARS

INGREDIENTS

450 g/1 lb preserving sugar
150 ml/5 fl oz red wine
  vinegar
750 g/1 lb 10½ oz ripe, juicy
  tomatoes, chopped
4 chillies (more if you like
  your chilli jam hot),
  seeded and chopped
3 garlic cloves, crushed
1 handful of oregano,
  finely chopped
Salt and pepper, to taste

METHOD

- Sterilize the three preserving jars by heating them in the oven (lids separate) for ten minutes at 140°C/275°F/ gas mark 1. Place a saucer in the refrigerator.
- Place the sugar and vinegar in a heavy-based saucepan (or preserving pan) and cook over a medium heat until the sugar has dissolved.
- Add the chopped vegetables and stir together in the pan. Boil vigorously at a roiling boil until setting point – around fifteen minutes. Keep stirring to prevent the mixture from sticking. Check whether the jam is going to set by placing a teaspoonful on the chilled saucer: if when cooled it holds its shape when you push it with your finger, it is ready. If not, boil it a little longer and check again.
- Add the chopped oregano, season the jam to taste and then transfer into the warm, sterilized jars.
- Seal with the lids, covering each lid with a disc of waxed paper, and allow to cool.
- If you can resist it, you can store this preserve for up to three months in a cool, dark cupboard. Keep it in the refrigerator once opened.

RED CABBAGE & REDCURRANT PICKLE

This is a marriage made in heaven in terms of the flavour combination, as well as the fruits and vegetables providing a splash of summer colour and contrasts of height and foliage in the display. Not only are pickles crunchy and colourful, but they are also easy to make and enliven the simplest of dishes – this recipe is a twist on the classic cabbage and redcurrant combination. Preserving your harvests in this way will allow you to enjoy your produce in autumn and winter when there is not such an abundance of fresh fruit and vegetables at your fingertips.

POT RECIPE

1 x packet of red cabbage 'Romanov' seed
1 x redcurrant 'Rovada'
6 x onion 'Red Ray' sets
1 x 100-cm/40-inch-long trough
Multipurpose or soil-based compost
General organic vegetable fertilizer

GROW ME

SOW IN EARLY SPRING; PLANT IN MID- TO LATE SPRING

- Start the red cabbage early: sow the seed evenly in a seed tray, covering with about 1 cm/½ inch of compost. Keep in a heated greenhouse or on a sunny windowsill and make sure the compost does not dry out. When the seedlings are large enough to handle, transplant the strongest singly into 9-cm/3½-inch pots to grow on.

- In mid- to late spring, prepare the trough in a sunny, sheltered spot. Plant the redcurrant in one corner and the onion sets in another corner in two rows – more snugly than you would in raised beds, leaving about 10 cm/4 inches between them. Make sure that their tips

are just poking out above the surface of the compost.

- Plant out two red cabbage seedlings, once their roots appear at the bottom of the pot, in the front of the trough. Water in well. Then water regularly and feed every two weeks thereafter.

- The redcurrant could stay in the trough for three years; scrape off the top 7–10 cm/3–4 inches of soil and add new compost mixed with fertilizer each spring. In the fourth year, repot it into a larger container or trim off a third of the roots and replant it in the same trough.

ROOM IN THE POT

Sow perpetual spinach, chard or calabrese to provide winter and early spring harvests, before re-sowing the trough with onion and red cabbage in the following spring.

TIME TO HARVEST

Harvest in late summer, when the redcurrants are ripe, the onion leaves have yellowed and the cabbages have bulked up.

EAT ME

RED CABBAGE & REDCURRANT PICKLE

MAKES TWO
1- LITRE/6-INCH JARS

INGREDIENTS
1 red cabbage, cored,
    quartered and shredded
1 red onion, sliced
150 g/5 oz salt
1 litre/35 fl oz vinegar
40 g/1½ oz pickling spice
2 tbsp soft brown sugar
2 handfuls of redcurrants

METHOD
- Sterilize two preserving jars by heating them in the oven (lids off) for ten minutes at 140°C/275°F/gas mark 1.
- Spread the cabbage and onions in a large bowl in layers, sprinkling each layer generously with salt; cover and place in the refrigerator overnight.
- Meanwhile, place the vinegar, pickling spice and sugar in a heavy-bottomed saucepan and slowly bring to the boil. Keep stirring until the sugar has dissolved. Turn off the heat and let the pickling liquid infuse overnight.
- The following morning, wash the salt off the cabbage and onion and pat dry with kitchen paper.
- Fill each jar with cabbage, onion and redcurrants. Strain the pickling liquid and pour it into the jars until it reaches the tops. Seal with the lids, covering each lid with a disc of waxed paper.
- Leave the pickle for a week or two in a cool, dry place before eating it (store it in the refrigerator after opening).

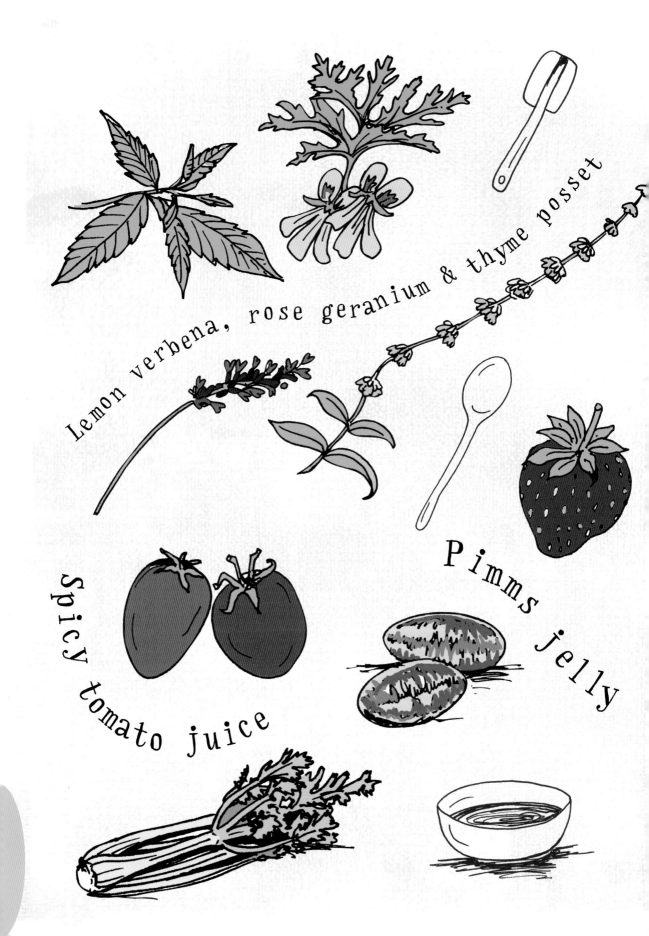

Lemon verbena, rose geranium & thyme posset

Spicy tomato juice

Pimms jelly

Strawberry smoothie

DRINKS & PUDS

Blueberry & rose geranium compote

LEMON VERBENA, ROSE GERANIUM & THYME POSSET

All the herbs in this pot produce flowers that are great for pollinating insects.

This heavily scented pot is best placed next to a seat or the front door so you can enjoy the fragrance all summer long. The combination of colours and textures in this pot work well too, with frothy lavender and compact, lilac-tinted thyme set against pale lime-coloured lemon verbena, the lush spires of lemon basil and the sculptural rose-geranium leaves. Infuse the leaves to make a syrup for a tangy lemon posset – the medieval pudding that is making something of a comeback!

POT RECIPE

1 x 1-litre/13-cm pot of lemon basil (*Ocimum x africanum*)
1 x 1-litre/13-cm pot of lemon verbena (*Aloysia citrodora*)
1 x 1-litre/13-cm pot of rose geranium
   (*Pelargonium* 'Graveolens')
2 x 1-litre/13-cm pot of *Thymus pulegioides* 'Foxley'
1 x 1-litre/13-cm pot of English lavender
   (*Lavandula angustifolia* 'Hidcote')
1 x 50-cm/20-inch-diameter container
Multipurpose or soil-based compost
General organic vegetable fertilizer
Horticultural grit

GROW ME

PLANT IN SPRING

- These herbs have the best flavour if grown in full sun, but give them a sheltered position. Fill the container with compost and fertilizers. Plant the lemon basil at the back of the container and the lemon verbena and rose geranium opposite each other across the middle of the pot, so the three herbs form the points of a triangle.
- Make two planting holes for the thymes on either side at the front of the pot and a planting hole for the lavender in-between them. Add a couple of handfuls of horticultural grit to the bottom of each planting hole. Water in all the herbs well.
- Pick the herbs regularly to encourage plenty of new growth and to maintain a neat habit.

TIME TO HARVEST

You can start picking the herbs regularly in early summer, once they have become established.

EAT ME   LEMON VERBENA, ROSE GERANIUM & THYME POSSET

SERVES FOUR

INGREDIENTS
Juice and zest of 1 lemon
150 g/5 oz caster sugar
2 leaves of lemon verbena
2 sprigs of lemon basil
2 leaves of scented geranium
1 long sprig of thyme
500 ml/18 fl oz double cream
1 handful of lavender florets

METHOD
- Place the lemon juice and zest in a small pan with the sugar over a low heat and bring gradually to the boil, stirring occasionally, until the sugar has dissolved.
- Add the lemon verbena, lemon basil and scented geranium leaves and the leaves from the thyme sprig (run your fingers downwards along the stem to remove the leaves from the stem). Leave the mixture to infuse, covered, for an hour.
- Pour the cream into a small, heavy-bottomed pan and stir gently until it comes to the boil. Pour it into the scented syrup, stirring well to mix it, then pour the mixture through a sieve into a jug. Discard the leaves.
- Divide the mixture between four 150-ml/5-fl oz glasses.
- Allow to cool completely, then refrigerate until set, usually two to three hours, or overnight.
- Sprinkle a few lavender florets and a young lemon verbena leaf over each posset just before serving them.

STRAWBERRY SMOOTHIE

Strawberries create the buzz in this display.

Smoothies are easy-peasy to make and are the bees' knees when it comes to fruit drinks. While pure juices have plenty of vitamins, their absence of fibre means their natural sugars are released quickly into the bloodstream to leave you feeling peckish before you know it. Smoothies, on the other hand, contain all the fruit's roughage so make our digestive systems work harder to break down the fibre. This means that the sugars are released more slowly into the body and you feel fuller for longer. Health benefits aside, the pink-flowered strawberry with the dark purple basil makes this a container pretty enough to take centre stage on a patio or balcony.

POT RECIPE

2 x strawberry 'Flamenco'
3 x strawberry 'Toscana' F1
1 x apple mint (*Mentha suaveolens*)
1 x basil (*Ocimum basilicum* 'Summer Surprise')
1 x 30-cm/12-inch-diameter container
Multipurpose or soil-based compost
General organic vegetable fertilizer

GROW ME

PLANT IN SPRING

- Set the container in a sunny, sheltered spot, then prepare it. Place the strawberries at equal distance around the edge of the pot, alternating varieties.
- Plant the mint in a 15-cm/6-inch pot and plunge the pot into the compost, leaving the rim of the pot above the surface. Mint is a bit of a thug, so this will help to restrict the roots and prevent it from taking over the container.
- Plant the basil in-between the mint and the front-most strawberries to make the most of the contrast in leaf colours.

- Water the container regularly to prevent it from drying out and feed the strawberries every week with a proprietary fertilizer. Remove the runners, cutting them off near the base, and pot them up to boost your stock or to give to friends and family. When strawberry flowers appear, add a straw layer as a mulch to avoid the fruits being splashed with compost and spoiling.
- Pick the basil and mint leaves regularly to promote new growth from the plants as well as a compact habit.

Both strawberry varieties, being perpetual types, crop from midsummer into early autumn and, of course, the herbs will be ready to harvest before that, so do not be bashful – use them whenever you can in salads, pasta and other dishes.

EAT ME

STRAWBERRY SMOOTHIE

SERVES TWO

INGREDIENTS
2 large handfuls of
    strawberries, hulled
1 small handful of mint
2 sprigs of basil
1 banana
1 tsp honey
Splash of water or apple juice

METHOD
- Put all the ingredients into a blender and blitz until smooth. Serve.

PIMMS JELLY

As well as being a twist on the popular summertime drink, this grown-up dessert is a seasonal showstopper. Use an old-fashioned jelly mould to make it more sumptuous.

The combination of strawberry and cucamelon flowers proves irresistible to pollinating insects.

2 x strawberry 'Flamenco'
1 x spearmint (*Mentha spicata*)
1 x packet of cucamelon (*Melothria scabra*) seed
1 x 45-cm/18-inch-diameter container
Multipurpose or soil-based compost
General organic vegetable fertilizer

GROW ME

SOW IN MID-SPRING; PLANT IN MID- AND LATE SPRING

- Position the prepared container in a sunny, sheltered spot in mid-spring and plant the strawberries, one to each side of the centre-front edge. Plunge-plant the mint in a 15-cm/6-inch pot (to restrict its roots) in the middle at the back.
- Lastly, prepare a 9-cm/3½-inch pot and thinly sow the cucamelon seed, covering it with 1 cm/½ inch of compost. Leave in a greenhouse or on a sunny windowsill to germinate.
- Once the seedlings are large enough (about 7 cm/3 inches) to handle and all risk of frost has passed, plant one cucamelon in the container – at the front in the gap between the strawberries, to allow the vine to trail over the side.
- Water regularly and feed with tomato fertilizer once the strawberry plants are in flower. Cut back the strawberry runners, so that the plants focus on producing a bountiful crop, and mulch with a layer of straw under the strawberry foliage, to prevent the compost from staining the fruits.
- Nip out the growing tip of the cucamelon once it reaches about 2.5 m/8 ft long and reduce its side shoots to about 40 cm/16 inches. Regularly pick the mint to keep it compact and stop it from taking over the container.

- At the end of the growing season, lift the cucamelon, repot it and leave in a frost-free, dry place, ready to plant out again in the following spring.

EAT ME

PIMMS JELLY

SERVES FOUR

INGREDIENTS
5 small leaves of gelatine
115 g/4 oz caster sugar
100 ml/3½ fl oz water
100 ml/3½ fl oz lemonade
175 ml /6 fl oz Pimms
250 g/9 oz strawberries,
   hulled and thinly sliced
4 cucamelons, thinly sliced
1 handful of mint leaves, sliced

METHOD
• Soak the gelatine leaves in cold
  tap water, leaving it for a few
  minutes to soften.
• Take a saucepan and dissolve
  the sugar in the water over a
  medium-low heat, stirring all
  the time. Take the pan off the
  heat and stir in the softened
  gelatine leaves.
• Transfer the mixture to a
  bowl and add the lemonade
  and Pimms. Leave to set,
  stirring occasionally.
• Once the jelly starts to set, add
  the strawberries, cucamelons
  and a little of the mint.
• Transfer into small glasses or
  a jelly mould and leave to set
  for at least four hours in the
  refrigerator before it is set and
  ready to serve. Garnish with
  the remaining mint leaves.

TIME TO HARVEST

The fruits of the cucamelon and
strawberries should be ripened
and ready to begin harvesting by
midsummer. You can pick the mint
leaves throughout the season.

BLUEBERRY & ROSE GERANIUM COMPOTE

Blueberry blossoms attract bees, butterflies and other pollinating insects.

Blueberries make a beautifully coloured compote and their subtle sweetness is enhanced by the delicate lemon-rose scent of the geranium leaf. They look great in a container: the textured leaves and soft pink flowers of the geraniums contrast nicely with the blueberry bushes, which look striking in autumn with their fiery foliage. Place near the house or on a patio. This compote is a godsend to have in the refrigerator, ready for you to create delicious dishes at the drop of a hat: pour a few generous spoonfuls over granola for a morning treat; spread it luxuriously in the middle of a sponge cake; or swirl it through thick vanilla or Greek yogurt for a popular pudding.

POT RECIPE

1 x blueberry 'Sutton's Early'
1 x blueberry 'Sutton's Late'
2 x rose geranium (*Pelargonium* 'Graveolens')
1 x 50-cm/20-inch-diameter container
Ericaceous (acid) compost
General organic vegetable fertilizer

GROW ME

PLANT IN LATE SPRING

- Fill the container with ericaceous compost – blueberries are lime-hating plants – and position in a sunny, sheltered spot. If the pot is in partial shade, the blueberries will fruit later and will not put on such a show of autumn colour; also the rose geranium will not have such a strong scent.
- In late spring, after the risk of frost has passed, plant the blueberries on either side towards the back of the container and space the geraniums at the front.
- Water regularly – if you can use rainwater collected in a water butt, all the better,

because tap water is often alkaline or 'hard' and raises the pH levels of the compost, adversely affecting the crop. Feed with a liquid fertilizer for lime-hating plants during the growing season. Take care that birds do not beat you to the fruit – you might need to net the pot.
- Both the rose geraniums and blueberries are perennial, so you can keep this container going for several years. They do need to be protected from winter cold and wet: bring the pot under cover if necessary.

Using early- and late-flowering blueberry varieties extends the harvesting season from midsummer to early autumn. The rose geranium leaves may be picked throughout the season; you can also use the edible flowers as decoration for summer dishes from mid- to late summer.

EAT ME

BLUEBERRY & ROSE GERANIUM COMPOTE

SERVES TWO

INGREDIENTS
300 g/10½ oz blueberries
6 rose geranium leaves and
   a few flowers
6 tbsp water
1 tbsp caster sugar

METHOD
- Put the blueberries, rose geranium leaves, water and sugar in a heavy-based saucepan. Heat gently, stirring; when the water starts steaming, turn down the heat and leave the berries to simmer and burst gently.
- When the blueberries have softened, remove the rose geranium leaves and allow the blueberries to cool.
- Serve with a yogurt as a healthy breakfast or pudding and garnish with a few geranium flowers.

SPICY TOMATO JUICE

Try something different with your tomato harvest and make this refreshing, healthy drink, which is just what you need to kick-start the weekend after a great Friday night out! The trick is to combine a late-cropping tomato with an early-cropping celery to make sure that you can harvest both vegetables at the same time. This is a good display, with lovely textures and lush green foliage, that will thrive in a sunny spot. Use the leafy tips of the celery in soups and salads too.

POT RECIPE

1 x packet of chilli 'Barak' seed
1 x packet of celery 'Golden Self-blanching 3' seed
1 x packet of tomato 'Guilietta' F1 seed
1 x 50-cm/20-inch-diameter container
Multipurpose or soil-based compost
General organic vegetable fertilizer

GROW ME   SOW IN EARLY AND MID-SPRING; PLANT IN EARLY SUMMER

- In early spring, sow a few chilli seeds into a 9-cm/3½-inch pot. Thin the seedlings to the strongest and grow on.
- In mid-spring, prepare a modular tray with seed compost. Sow the celery and tomato seed in separate rows of the tray, two seeds per cell, and cover with 1 cm/½ inch or so of compost. Leave in a heated greenhouse or on a sunny windowsill. Prick out when the seedlings are large enough to handle into individual 9-cm/3½-inch pots to grow on.
- In early summer, plant up the prepared container in a sheltered, sunny spot. It is a good idea to position the single tomato at the back of the container, with two celery plants lined up in front of it and

one chilli plant placed in front of the celery. At the same time put in a cane to support the tomato as it grows.
- Water the growing vegetables well and do not let the soil dry out. Feed every two weeks with a tomato fertilizer once the tomato and chilli flowers set. Pinch out the side shoots of the tomato as it grows and stake the chilli once its fruits start to appear.

EAT ME

SPICY TOMATO JUICE

SERVES ONE

INGREDIENTS
3 celery sticks
150 g/5 oz tomatoes, chopped
1 chilli, deseeded and cut finely
Juice of half a lemon
Salt and pepper, to taste

METHOD
- Use a juicer to extract the celery juice and add the liquid to a blender.
- Add the remaining ingredients and blitz until smooth. It is ready to drink!

TIME TO HARVEST

Wait until late summer when the celery is ready to start harvesting, the tomatoes are really ripe and the chillies are fiery too.

USEFUL ADDRESSES

POT AND CONTAINER SUPPLIERS

Apta
Dencora Way
Leacon Road
Fairwood Business Park
Ashford
Kent
TN23 4FH
Tel: 01233 621090
Website: www.apta.co.uk

Burgon & Ball
La Plata Works
Holme Lane
Sheffield
S6 4JY
Tel: 0114 2338262
Website: www.burgonandball.com

Cadix Ltd
Unit 6
Two Counties Industrial Estate
Falconer Road
Haverhill
Suffolk
CB9 7XZ
Tel: 01440 713704
Website: www.cadix.co.uk

Crocus Ltd
Nursery Court
London Road
Windlesham
Surrey
GU20 6LQ
Tel: 01344 578000
Website: www.crocus.co.uk

Foras
West Head
Stow Bridge
King's Lynn
Norfolk
PE34 3NJ
Tel: 01366 381069
Website: www.foras.co.uk

Garden Trading
Carterton South Industrial Estate
Carterton
Oxfordshire
OX18 3EZ
Tel: 0845 6084448
Website: www.gardentrading.co.uk

Iota Garden and Home Ltd
Wick Road
Wick St Lawrence
North Somerset
BS22 7YQ
Tel: 01934 522617
Website: www.iotagarden.com

Ivy Line
Global House
High Street
Keresley
Coventry
CV6 2EN
Tel: 0844 8002214
Website: www.ivylinegb.co.uk

Primrose
44 Portman Road
Reading
RG30 1EA
Tel: 0118 9035210
Website: www.primrose.co.uk

The Stewart Company
Beaumont Road
Banbury
Oxon
OX16 1RH
Tel: 0203 6575230
Website: www.stewartcompany.co.uk

Woodlodge Products Ltd
Babdown Airfield
Tetbury
Gloucestershire
GL8 8YL
Tel: 01666 501000
Website: www.woodlodge.co.uk

SEEDS, PLUGS AND PLANTS

Jekka's Herb Farm
Rose Cottage
Shellards Lane
Alveston
Bristol
BS35 3SY
Tel: 01454 418878
Website: www.jekkasherbfarm.com

Organic Plants
Delfland Nurseries Ltd
Benwick Road
Doddington
March
Cambridgeshire
PE15 0TU
Tel: 01354 740553
Website: www.delfland.co.uk

Rocket Gardens
Treverry Farm
Mawgan
Helston
Cornwall
TR12 6BD
Tel: 01326 222169
Website: www.rocketgardens.co.uk

Sarah Raven's Kitchen Garden
1 Woodstock Court
Blenheim Road
Marlborough
SN8 4AN
Tel: 0845 0920283
Website: www.sarahraven.com

Suttons Seeds
Woodview Road
Paignton
Devon
TQ4 7NG
Tel: 0333 4002899
Website: www.suttons.co.uk

Trehane Nursery
Stapehill Road
Wimborne
Dorset
BH21 7ND
Tel: 01202 873490
Website: www.trehane.co.uk

COMPOST SUPPLIERS

Bulrush Horticulture Ltd
Newferry Road
Bellaghy
Magherafelt
Co. Londonderry
BT45 8ND
Tel: 0287 9386555
Website: www.bulrush.co.uk

Carbon Gold
Hanover House
First Floor
Queen Charlotte Street
Bristol
BS1 4EX
Tel: 0117 2440032
Website: www.carbongold.com

VINTAGE GARDEN TOOLS AND EQUIPMENT

The Foodie Bugle Shop
Bincknoll House
Royal Wootton Bassett
SN4 8QR
Tel: 01793 852272
Website: www.thefoodiebugleshop.com

INDEX

page numbers in italics refer to captions

PLANTS

ACKNOWLEDGMENTS

Jason and I would like to thank the team at Frances Lincoln for asking us to do this book. Thanks to Helen and Andrew for your guidance and Becky and Liz for your brilliant expertise.

Silvana, we are both hugely grateful to you for your positivity and energy in transforming our pot-grown crops into delicious recipes . . . the de Soissons are a crack team! Thanks too for your generosity with The Foodie Bugle Shop's stock – what a prop house. We cannot wait to visit your shop in Bath and get our hands on more gorgeous vintage kitchenalia!

I would like to thank Fran at Rabbit Attack PR for your boundless enthusiasm and for giving the green light to the idea of me and twenty-five pots 'moving in' to the polytunnels at Suttons. Toby, if only you had known what you were getting into! Thanks for your patience, support and sense of humour: I could not have done this without you and I am eternally grateful. Thanks to Ros and the boys at the trial grounds too.

A special thank you to Annelise for her wonderful attention to detail: Lord knows it was necessary.

Mum, thanks for supplying the best crocks I have ever seen and making the tastiest sandwiches I have ever eaten! And thank you for helping me to get all the pots sown and planted: it was great fun doing that together and I will always treasure our 'pot days'.

Dad, thanks for being happy to play golf while Mum was with me and for looking after Teddy.

Chef Paul Collins, thank you for coming to the rescue and finding me a beautiful copy of *Larousse Gastronomique*!

Hal, my darling, thanks for being a brilliant co-pilot as we rattled around the countryside in the 'flower-van' and to my gorgeous husband Jason, thanks as always for making everything look so beautiful.